GUILLERMO SRODEK-HART **STORIES**

With Texts by Anne Wilkes Tucker
and Guillermo Srodek-Hart

Prestel
Munich · London · New York

El Zorro 2005 6

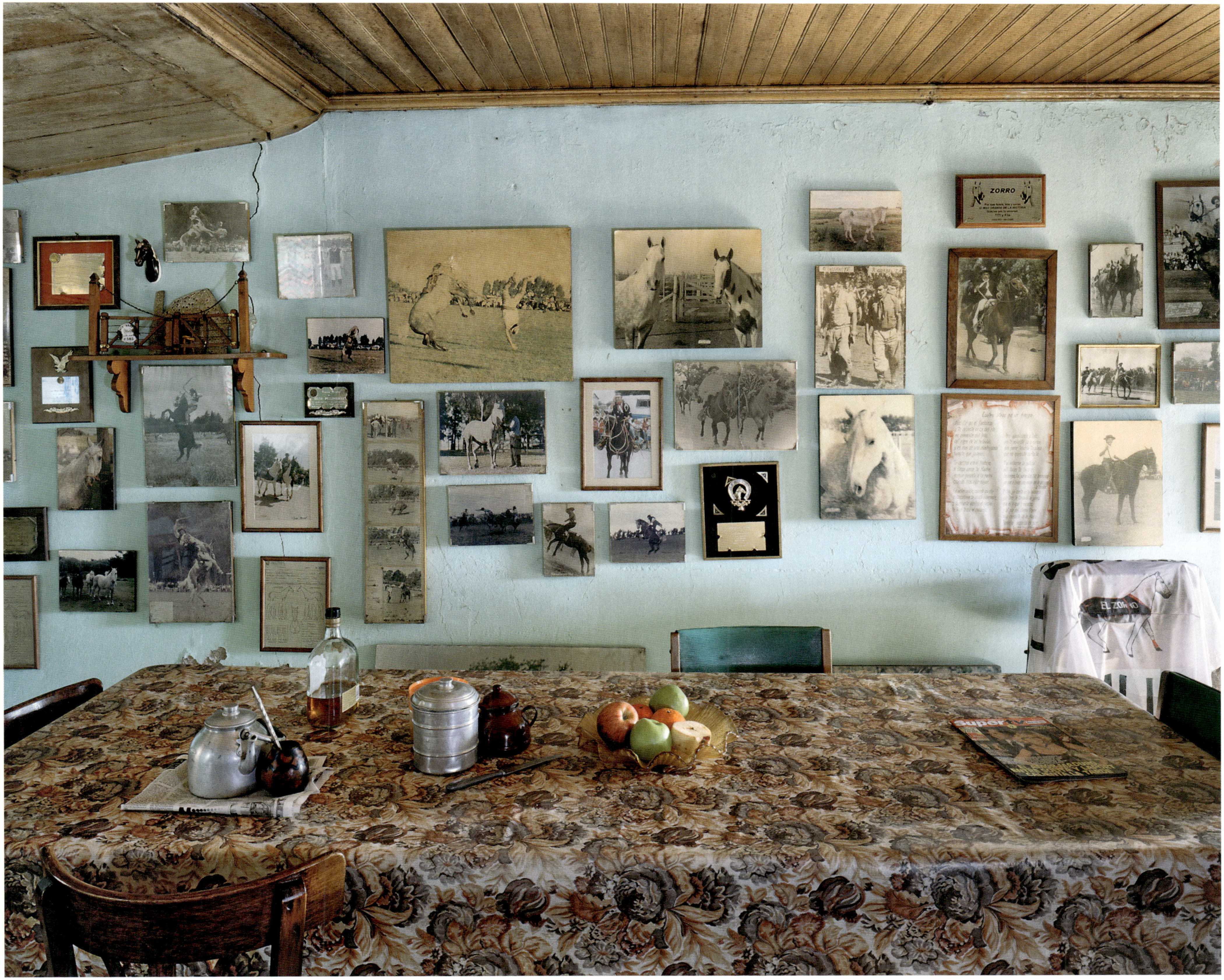
ZORRO
EL ZORRO
Super

Vernacular Visions

Anne Wilkes Tucker

Rushing along country roads precludes discovery; and if a list of "sites not to be missed" exists, burn it, because that is a record of someone else's adventure. Instead, bring curiosity, an open mind, and a capacity to wander aimlessly, at least in the early days of the route. For ten years, Guillermo Srodek-Hart roamed over thousands of kilometers of remote country roads in Argentina, stopping in small towns, at isolated dwellings, and in front of buildings lacking any remotely modern details. Think of Alice's adventure when she fell through the rabbit hole, or Owen Wilson's character Gil in the movie *Midnight in Paris* when he is mysteriously transported into earlier Parisian decades. Srodek-Hart did not meet any mad queens, but he is now acquainted with a head-shrinker (of the physical not mental kind). More like the fictional Gil, he met artisans with skills more common in other eras, and he found types of businesses long since replaced elsewhere by chain stores. As he began to photograph, the project's focus slowly became the interiors of these small business, some of which were no longer functioning but left with dust-laden merchandise undisturbed by the passage of considerable time. Other establishments were still selling handmade products. These interiors included one with jumbles of ostrich feet and animal horns awaiting transformation into knife handles in Tres Arroyos and neat stacks of components for constructing brooms in Chivilcoy (pp. 101 and 129). He also found beautifully handcrafted and carefully polished wooden cabinets and bars, outdated technologies, and wildly incongruous displays of goods, some neatly arrayed and others stacked higgledy-piggledy. The bars and eateries included games that were not digital (and not even electric), the inevitable portraits of local sports teams, mounted hunting trophies, and great varieties of long-necked bottles lined up like soldiers on narrow shelves. These predominantly one-person operations employ human craft, not programmed automation, and personal, not corporate, visions of organization and inventory. Srodek-Hart also documented the workplaces of other professions, including those of welders, butchers, cobblers, dry cleaners, grocers, bakers, rope makers, mechanics, pharmacists, and, most frequently, bartenders and general storekeepers. Proprietors appear in a small percentage of the pictures, and all of them are elderly. Many of the shops have closed since the beginning of the project.

Srodek-Hart's work exists within a long photographic tradition dating to one of the earliest existing photographs by Nicéphore Niépce of a still-life display in his studio. Others in this documentary tradition, whom Srodek-Hart cites as influences, include Eugène Atget and Martín Chambi. A more direct and personal lineage can be traced from Walker Evans to Evans's onetime printer Jim Dow to Srodek-Hart, who studied with Dow and Bill Burke at the School of the Museum of Fine Arts, Boston, and then worked as Dow's assistant. In his book *American Photographs*, Evans worked from a deep and broad ambition to convey America in its ascendancy while struggling through the Great Depression. Working with an 8×10-inch camera in the 1930s, Evans photographed rural and urban localities in the United States with a particular genius for recognizing the unadorned beauty of vernacular objects and spaces.[1] For decades, Dow has also focused on vernacular architecture in all kinds of hybrid formations, initially photographing in black and white like Evans and then switching to color to better capture the eye-catching paint and light combinations on some of his discoveries. Like Evans and Dow, Srodek-Hart looks for "humble beauty," particularly in less-visited regions, but Evans looked both for modern signs of progress, such as industries and their waste residue, and for historical buildings and monuments. Srodek-Hart is less ruthlessly classical in his style and allows an edge of nostalgia in his search for these residual architectures and shops from bygone times in Argentina. Having lived in the United States for eight years while in college and graduate school, he wanted to reconnect to what he associated with the Argentina of his youth. For instance, mention the knife maker and he talks about the gauchos of the Pampas who can "never leave the ranch house without a knife."[2] The knife maker's ostrich feet and armadillo tails, he says, "are what touch me about the rural world." He also admires the totality of skills required by sole-ownership businesses, such as those of the artisan who skins animal carcasses and cures the leather to make saddles, belts, and lassos, or those of the butcher who slaughters animals in his backyard and cuts the

[1] I am indebted to the exhibition catalogue *On the Road: A Legacy of Walker Evans*, Robert Lehman Art Center, Brooks School (North Andover, Mass., 2010) for observations about Evans, and particularly to Belinda Rathbone's essay "All Gone to Look for America."

[2] Guillermo Srodek-Hart, e-mail to the author, June 30, 2014.

meat for his shop in San Jorge, a town with fewer than two hundred inhabitants. Like Evans and Dow, Srodek-Hart looks at the changes that economic and political forces have generated in the physiognomy of places, but these businesses are on the decline and may soon be extinct. "The notion of disappearing worlds," he notes, "is a worldwide issue."[3] His intent is to preserve a trace of it.

[3] Ibid.

I am drawn to these pictures by their formal beauty, the intelligence of the observations, and the coherency of the series, and because I also grew up in a culture of small shops whose owners were known to me, all of which are gone now. Home Depot has replaced the hardware store in which aisles were lined with barrels of nails and open containers of seeds and grain. I remember its dominant smells were of metal, musk, and men. Conversations there were not brisk. One began with personal questions before shifting to purpose. At cotton gins, which I visited with my uncle, initially there was no conversation at all. The men sat in metal chairs or squatted, leaning back against aged wooden walls, and looked at the sky or cotton fields for what seemed like an eternity to a child. These men regularly used and collected good knives and guns for work and hunting, and appreciated well-made tools. They would have wanted to handle every knife in the case in El Ombú Fodder Shop, measuring the knives' balance, the way the handles fit their hands, and the sharpness of the blades (p. 45). Although my family did not stuff the animals they hunted, plenty of people we knew did. Taxidermy also seems to be popular in Argentina. It took me a while, however, to notice the black wildcat perched on the knife case as well as the carancho[4] protruding above the coils of rope in the shop in Saladillo. Just as the trips taken to discover these stores required patience and keen observation, so do the photographs, or one will miss the pleasures of Srodek-Hart's adventures and discoveries.

[4] A carancho, also known as a caracara, is a bird of prey in the falcon family.

Bar Tito 2013

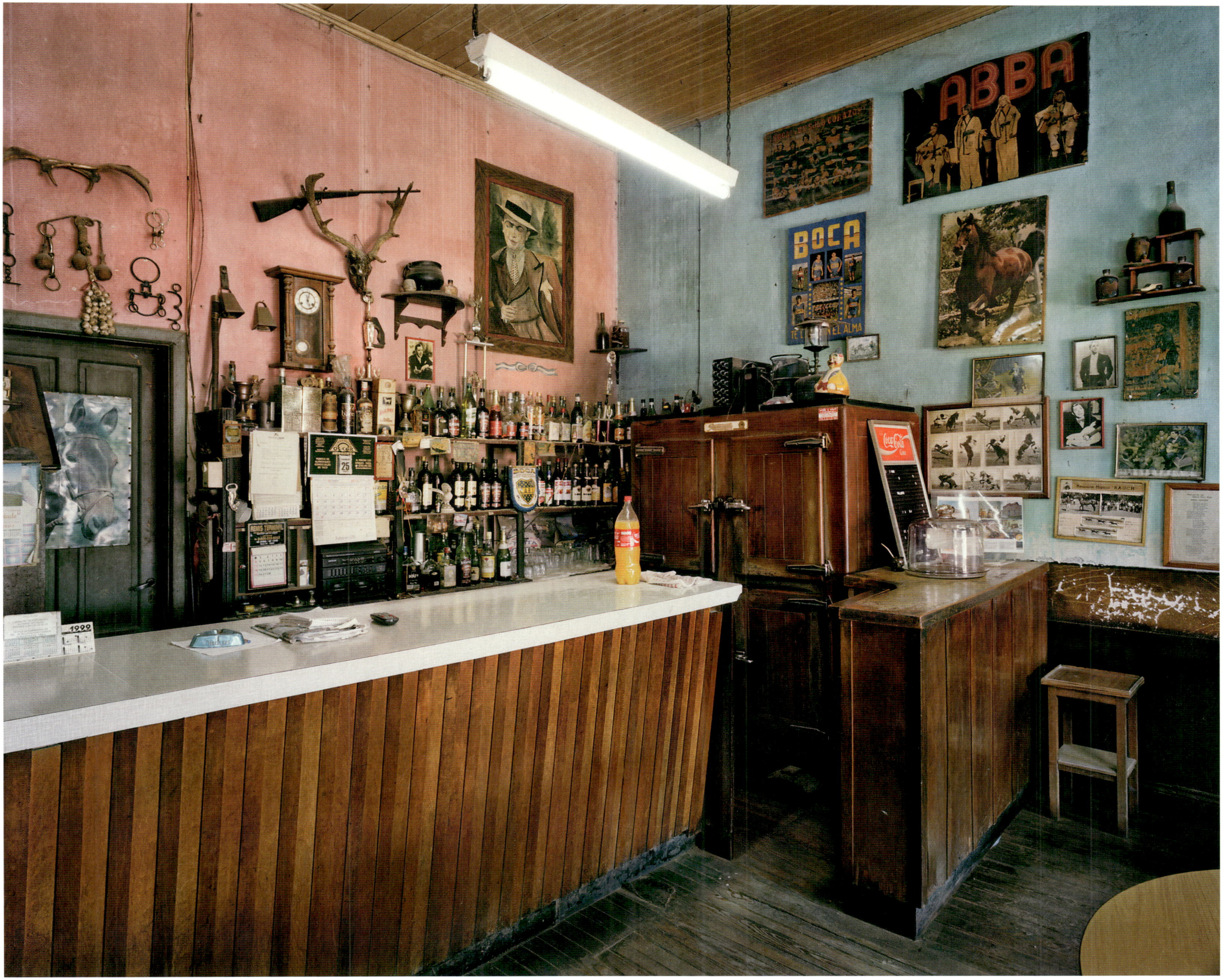
ABBA
BOCA
1999

Bar El Mate 2010 14

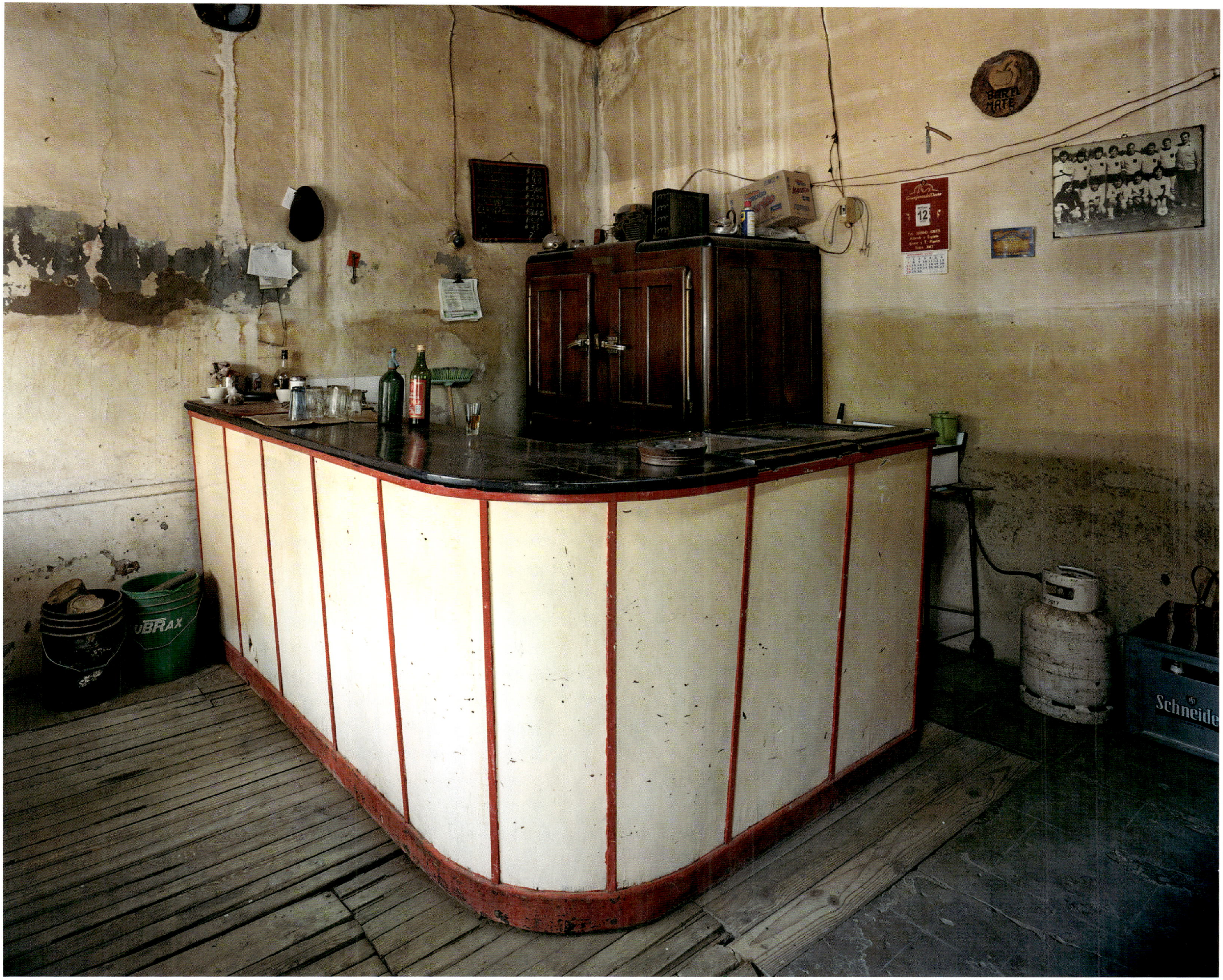
BAR EL MATE
UBRAX
Schneide

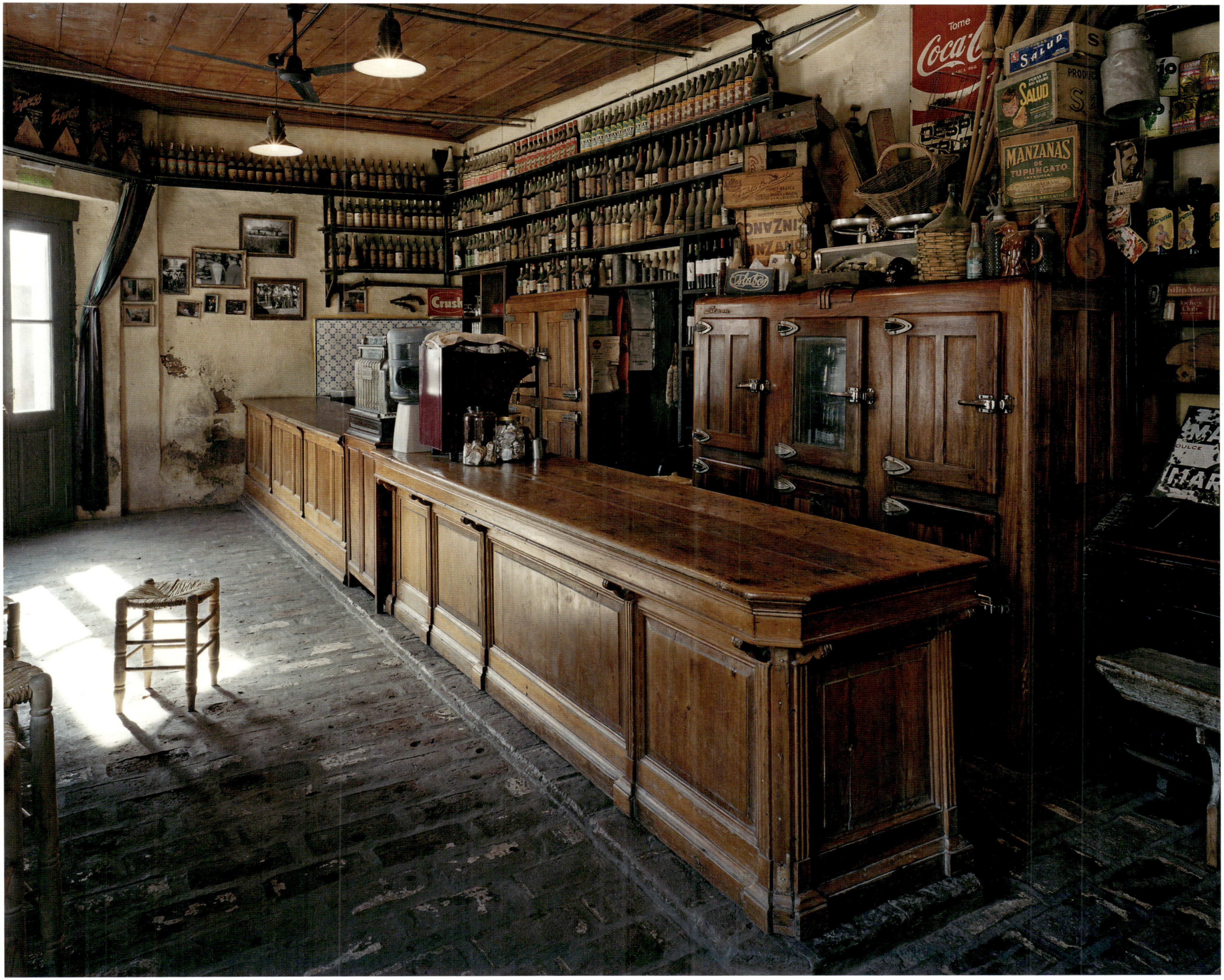
Tome
Coca-Cola
SALUD
SALUD
MANZANAS
DE
TUPUNGATO
Crush

Bar Melón 2014

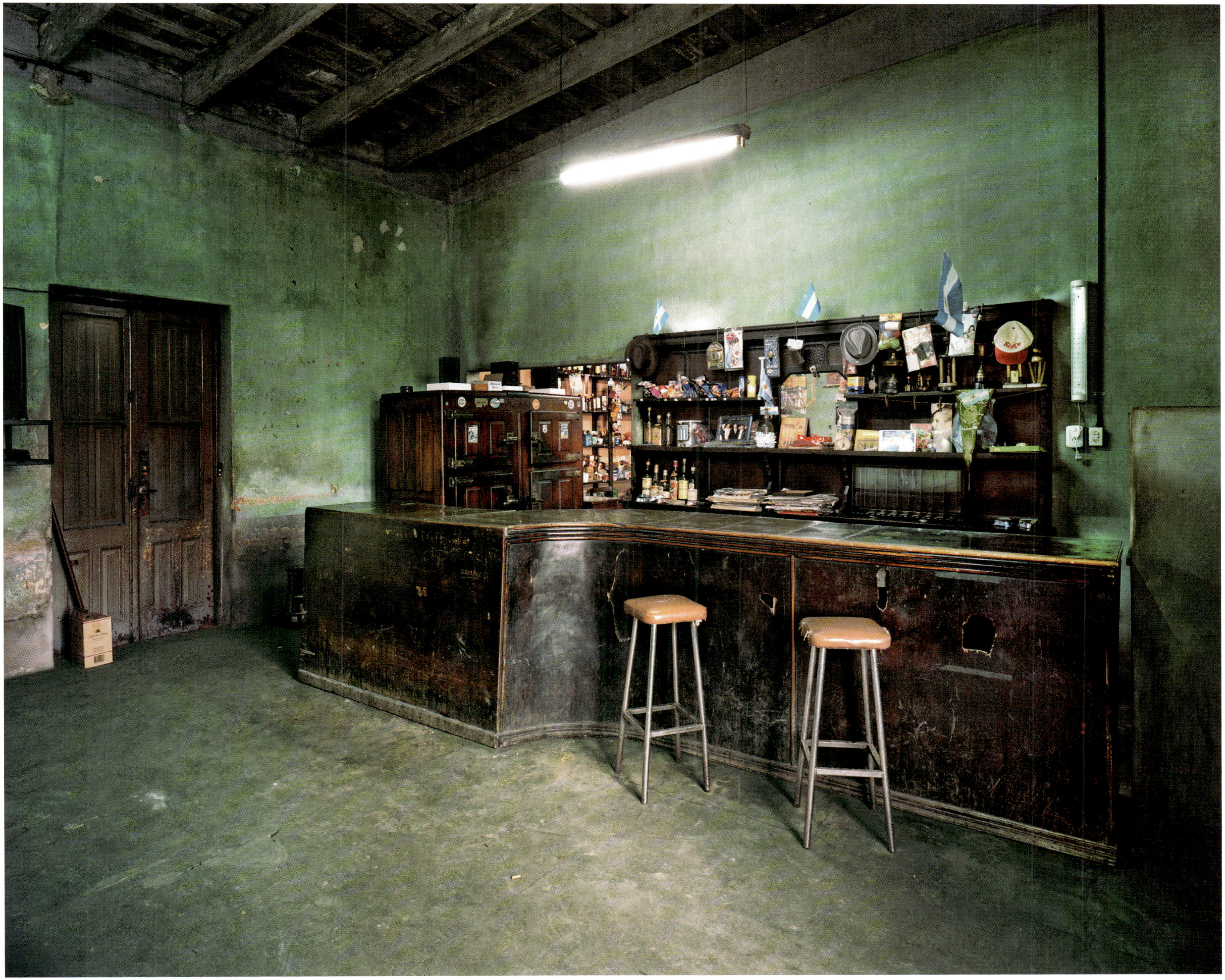

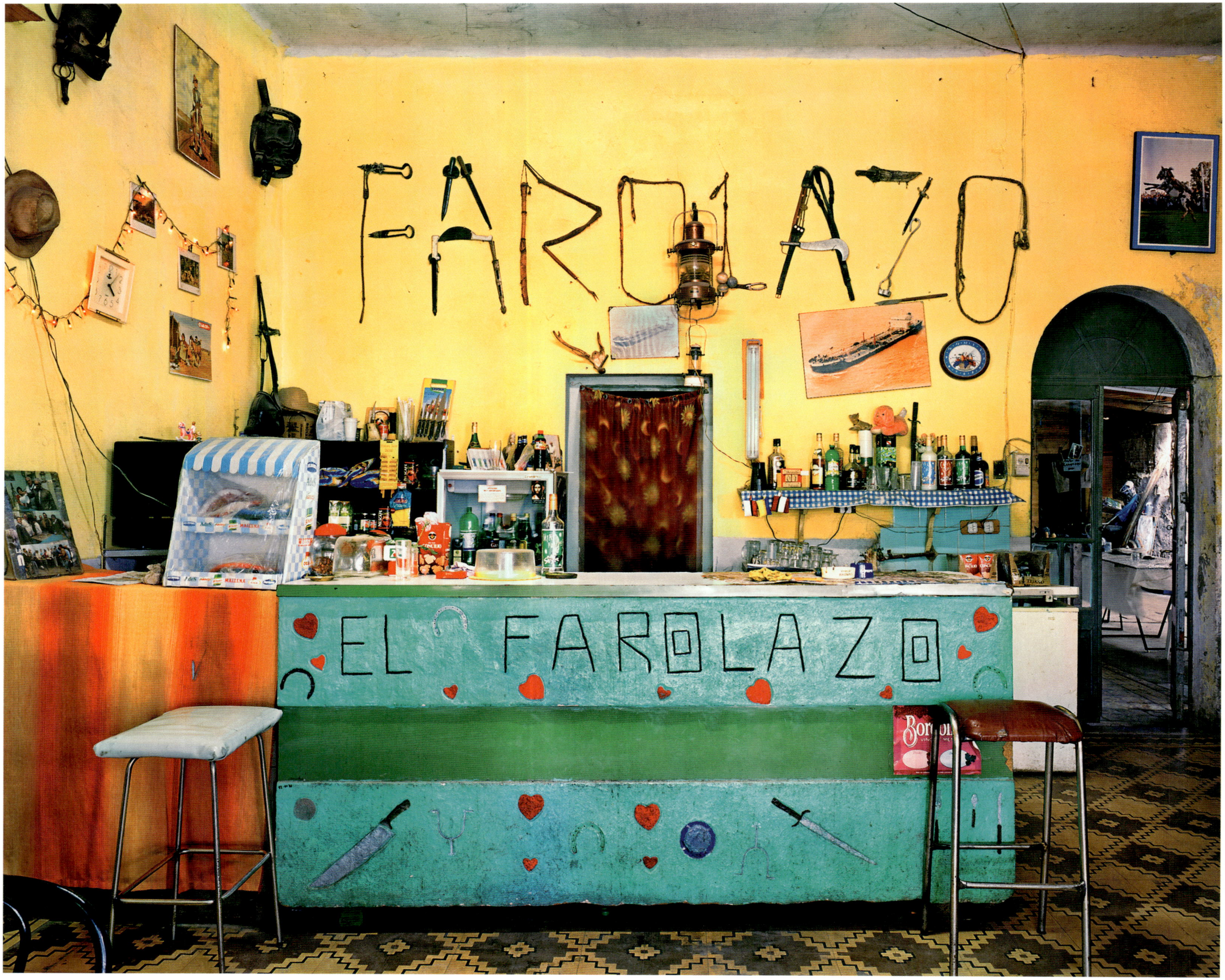
FAROLAZO
EL FAROLAZO

21 **El Farolazo** 2006

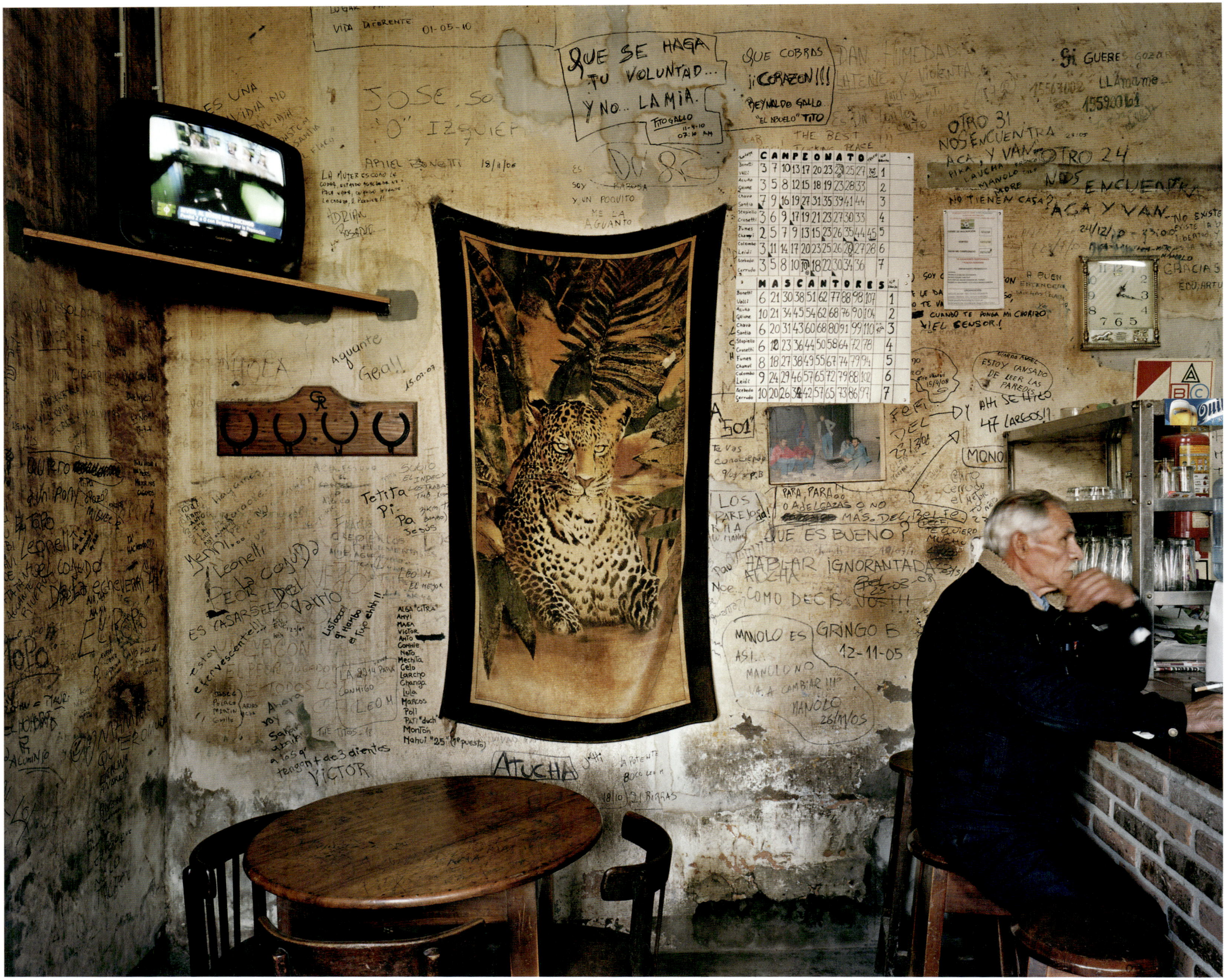

VIDA DIFERENTE 01-05-10
QUE SE HAGA TU VOLUNTAD... Y NO... LA MIA.
QUE COBRAS ¡¡CORAZON!!!
REYNALDO GALLO "EL ABUELO" TITO
CAMPEONATO
MASCANTORES
OTRO 31 NOS ENCUENTRA ACA Y VAN
OTRO 24 NOS ENCUENTRA ACA Y VAN
QUE ES BUENO?
HABLAR IGNORANTADA
MANOLO ES ASI
GRINGO E 12-11-05
ATUCHA
VICTOR

23 **El Tropezón** 2011

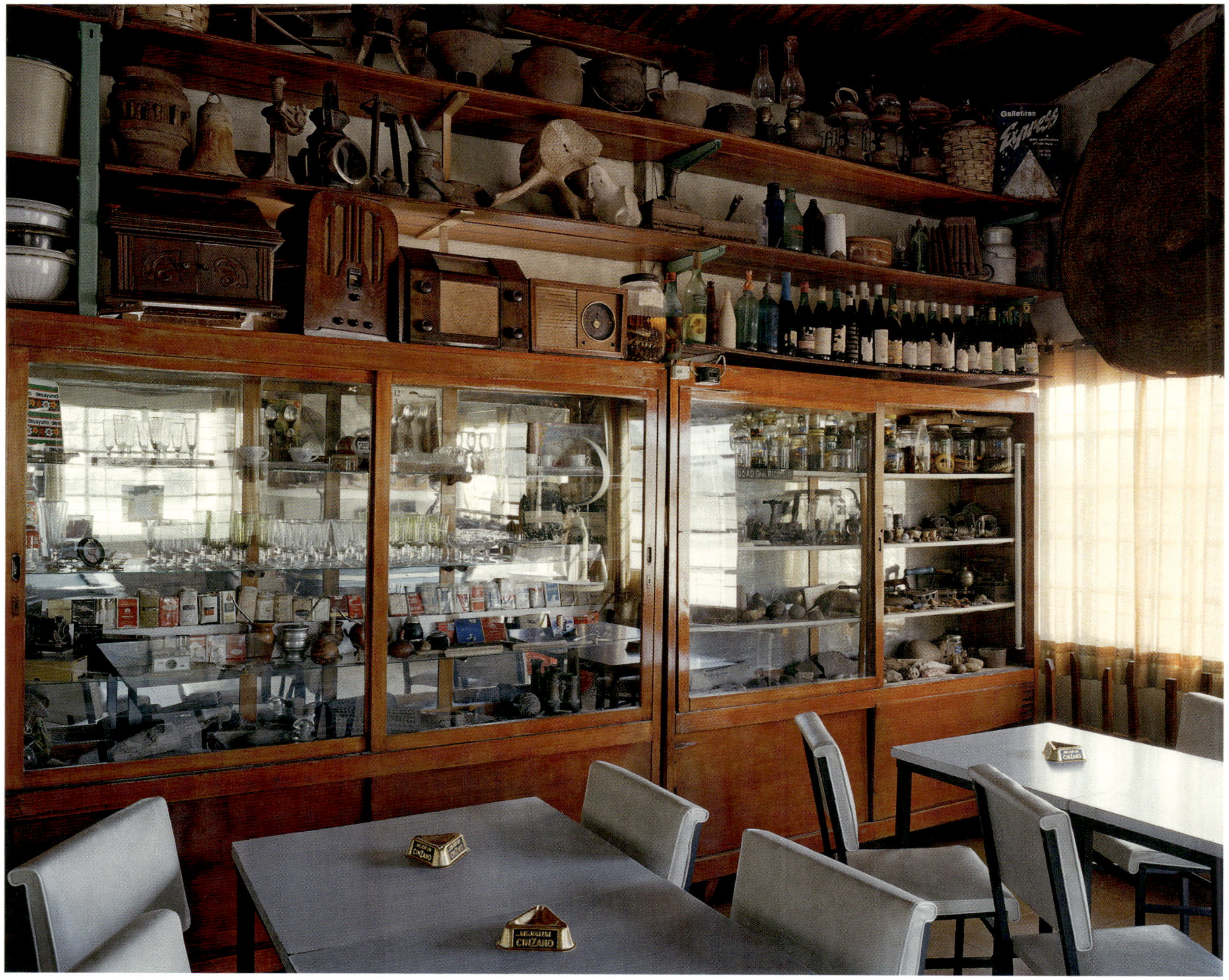

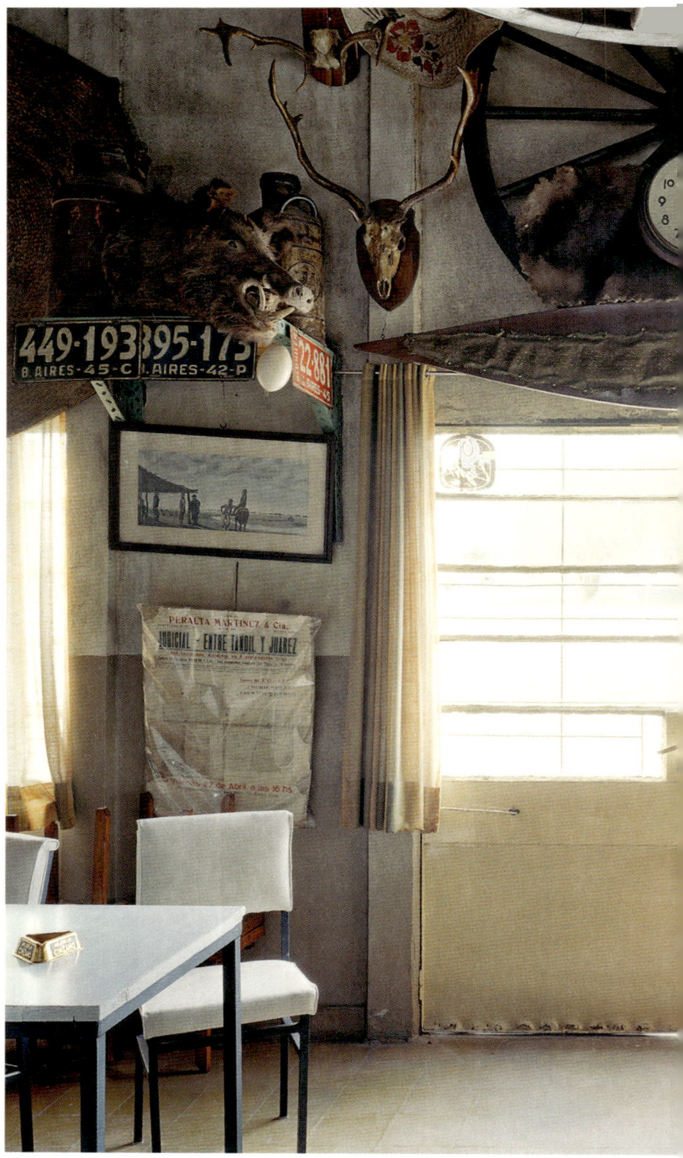
449-193
B. AIRES-45-C
395-175
AIRES-42-P

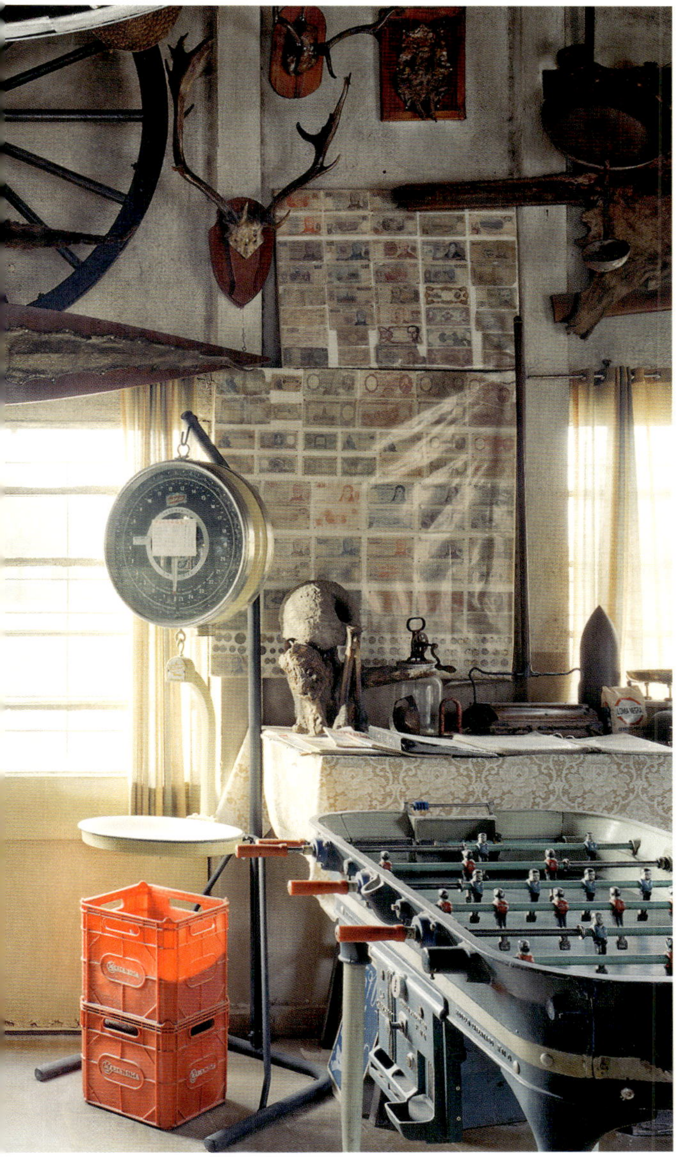

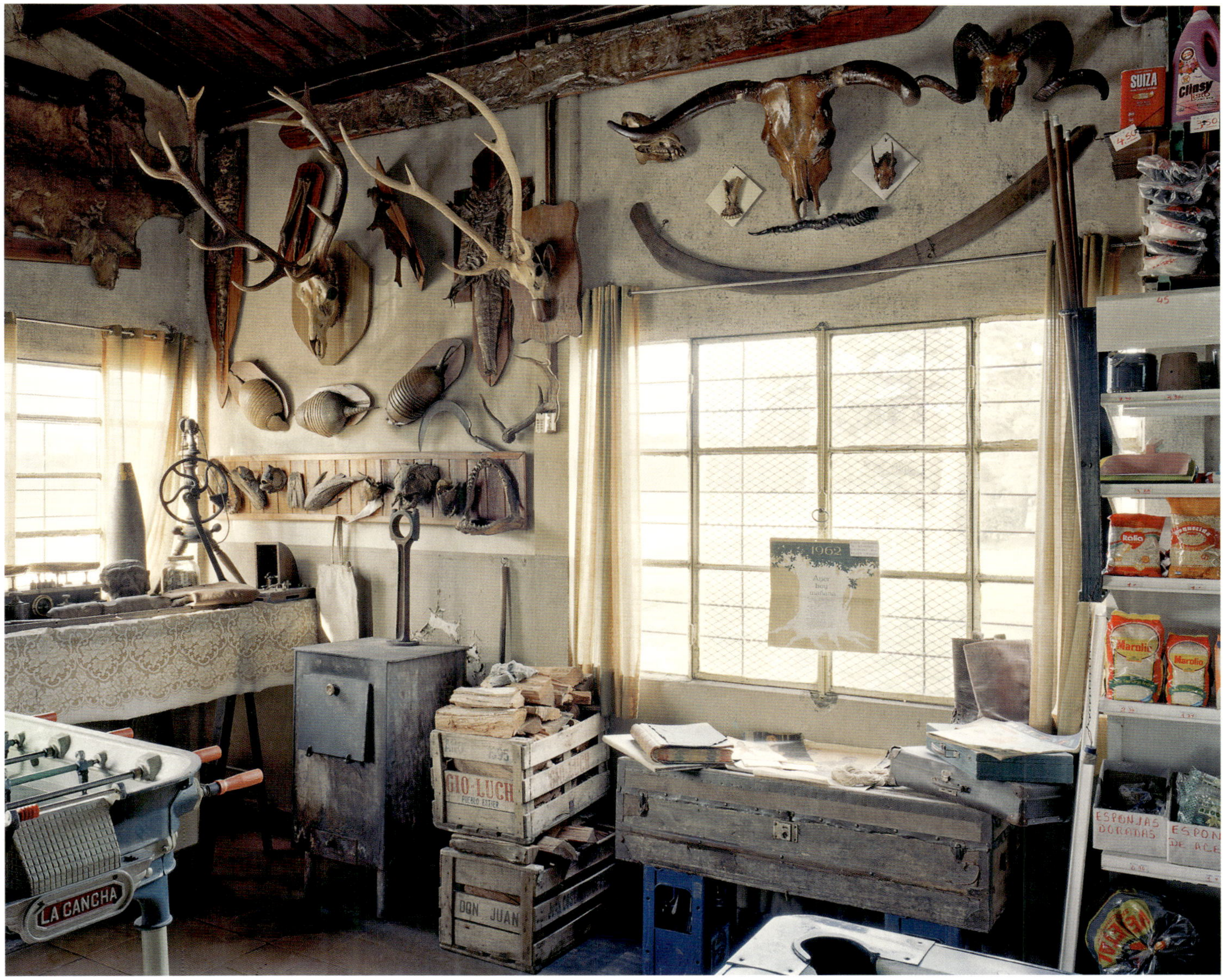
SUIZA
1962
GIO-LUCH
DON JUAN
LA CANCHA
ESPONJAS DORADAS
Marolio

Bar Cacique 2005

Cuatro Esquinas 2013

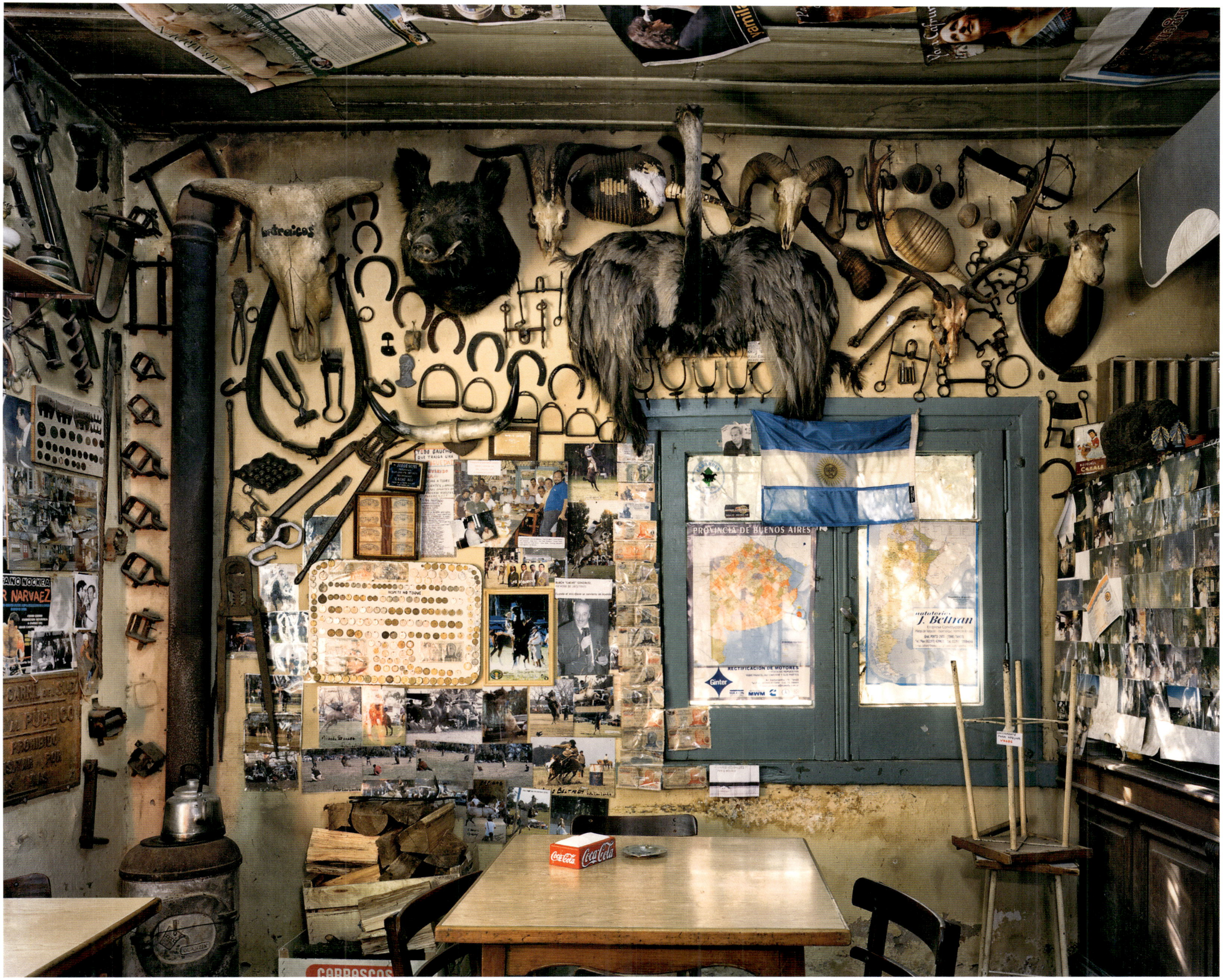
PROVINCIA DE BUENOS AIRES
RECTIFICACION DE MOTORES
Ginter
MWM
J. Beltran
Coca-Cola
Coca-Cola

Mira-Mar General Store 2014 28

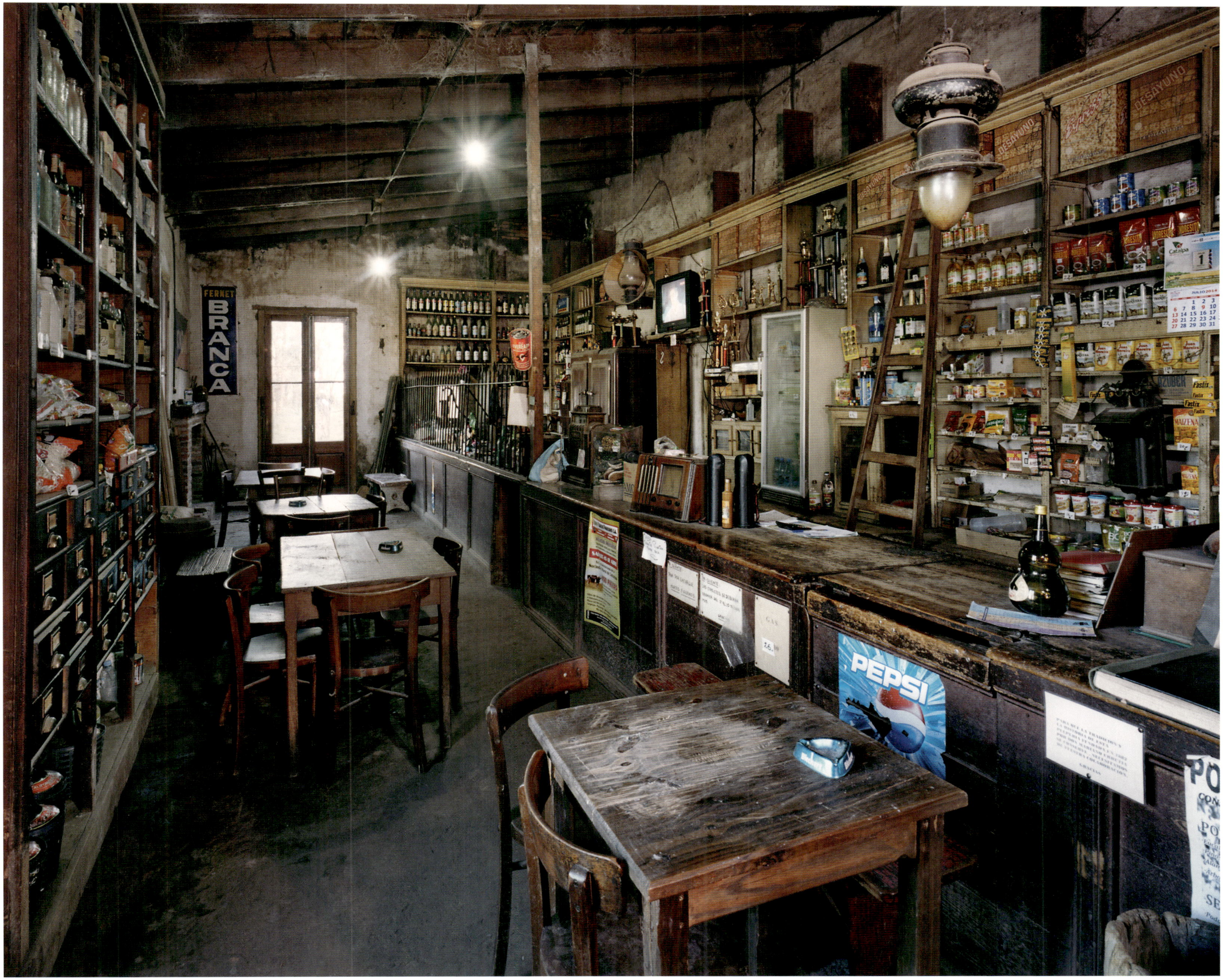
FERNET
BRANCA
PEPSI
DESAYUNO

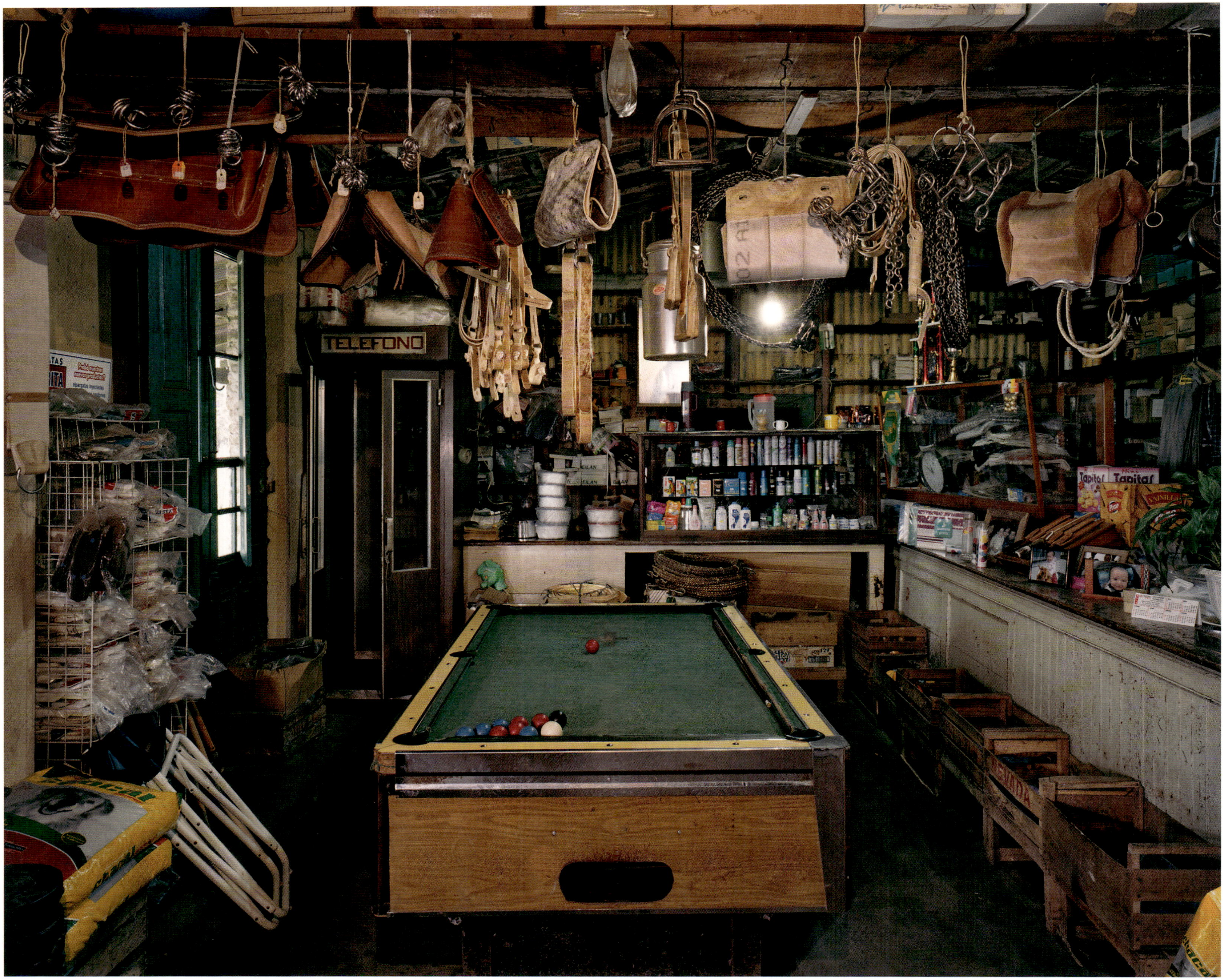
TELEFONO

31

Langueyú General Store 2013

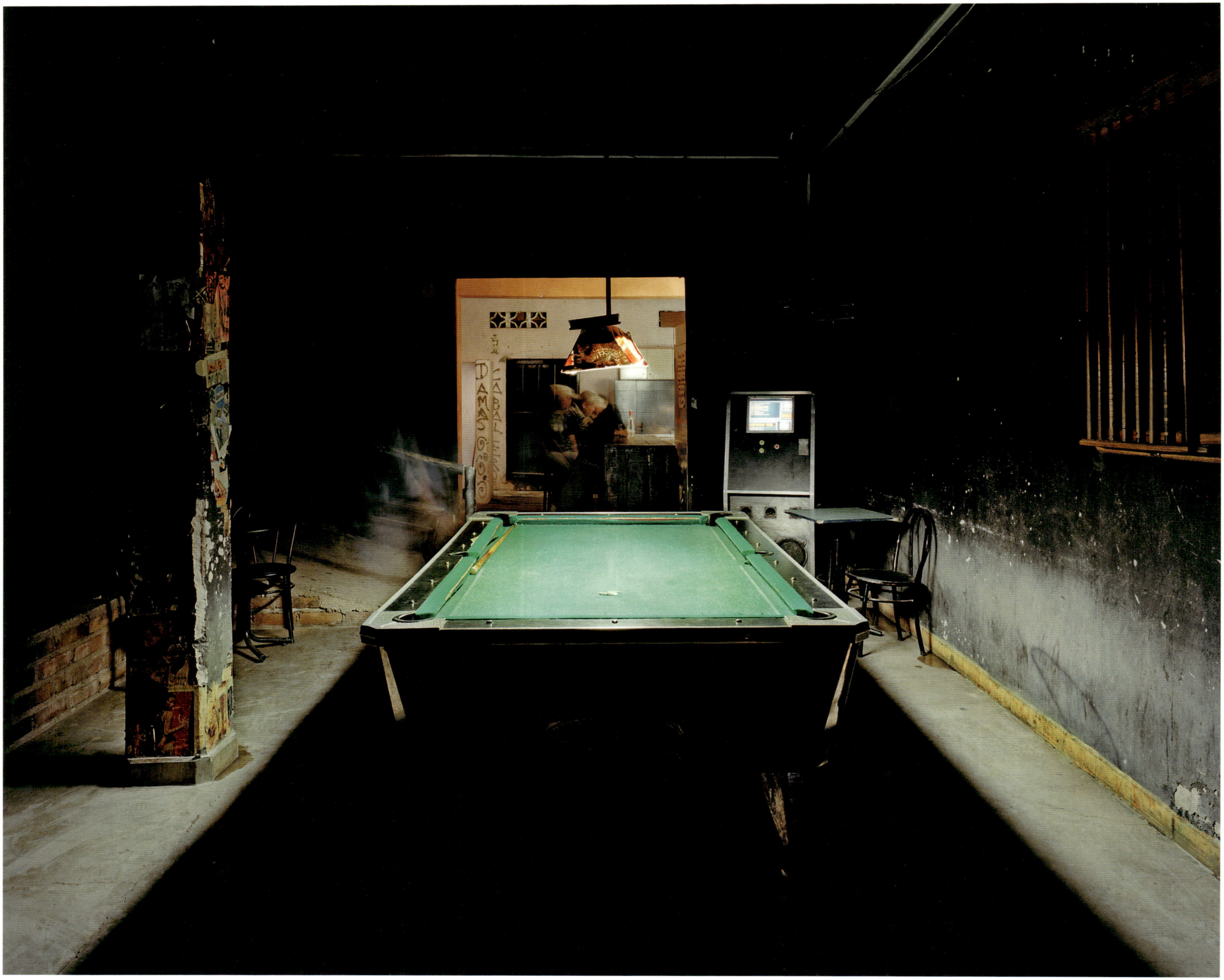
DAMAS

33 **Chilecito Pool Table** 2010

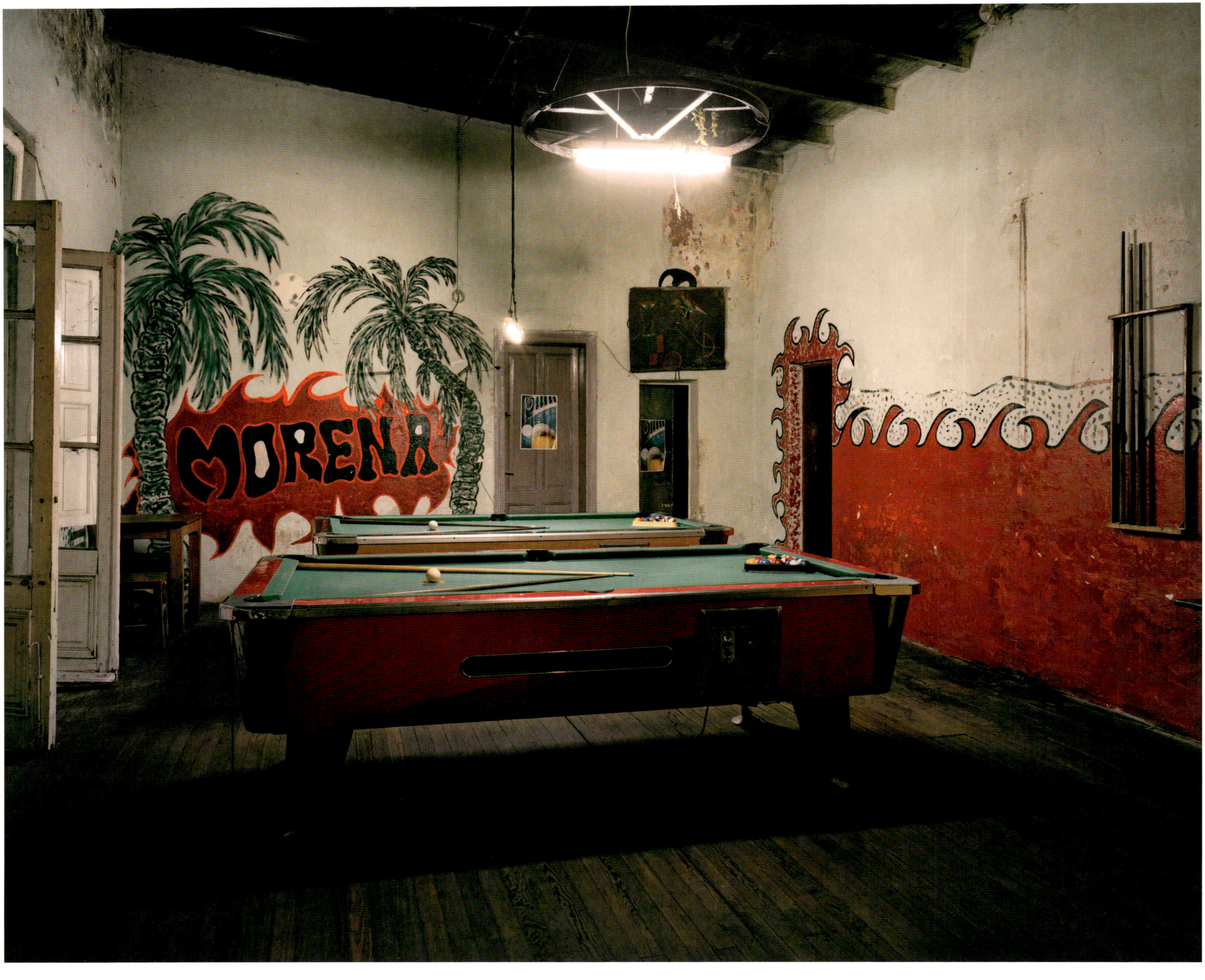
MORENA

35 **Bar Morena** 2011

Bar Mangioni 2010 36

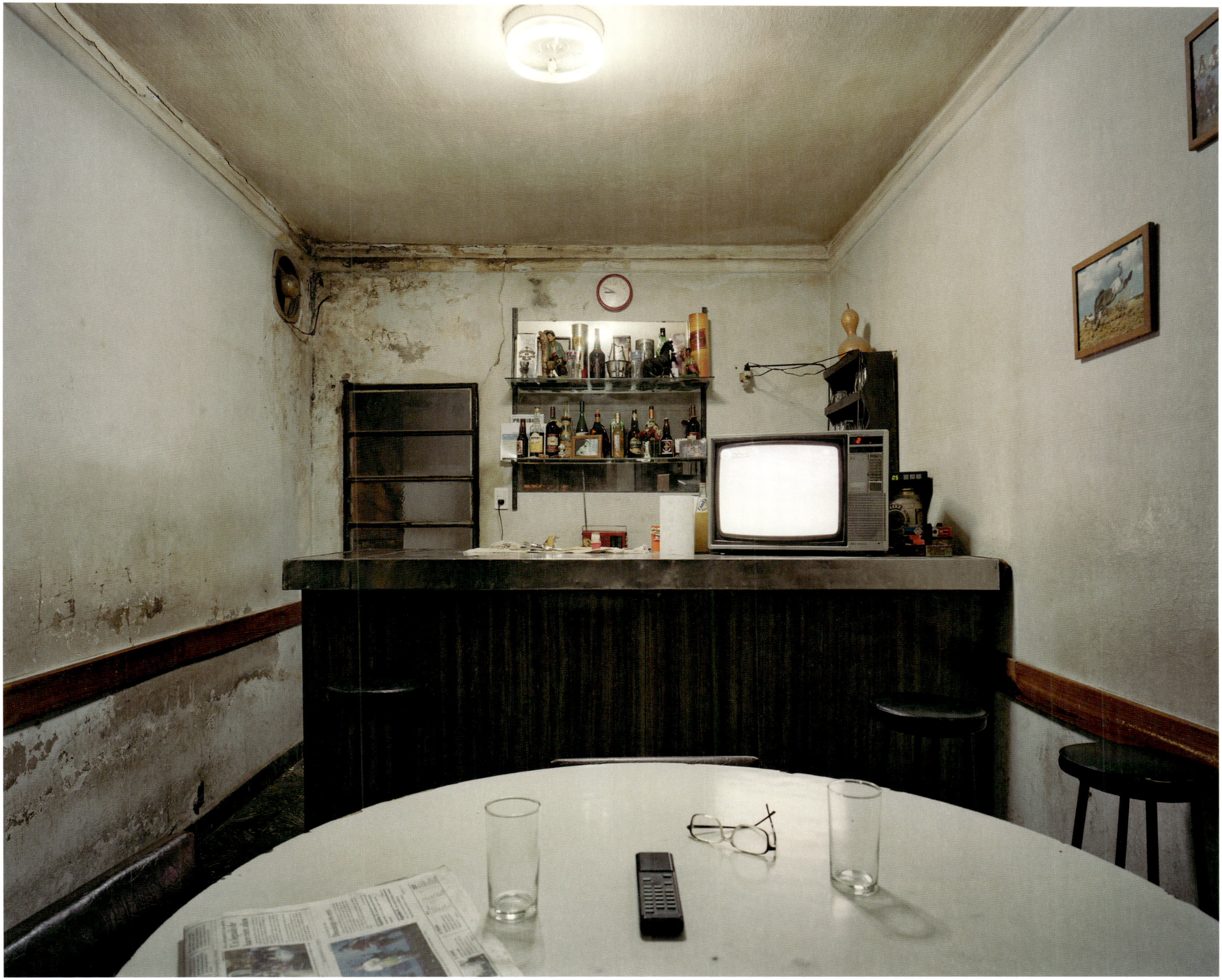

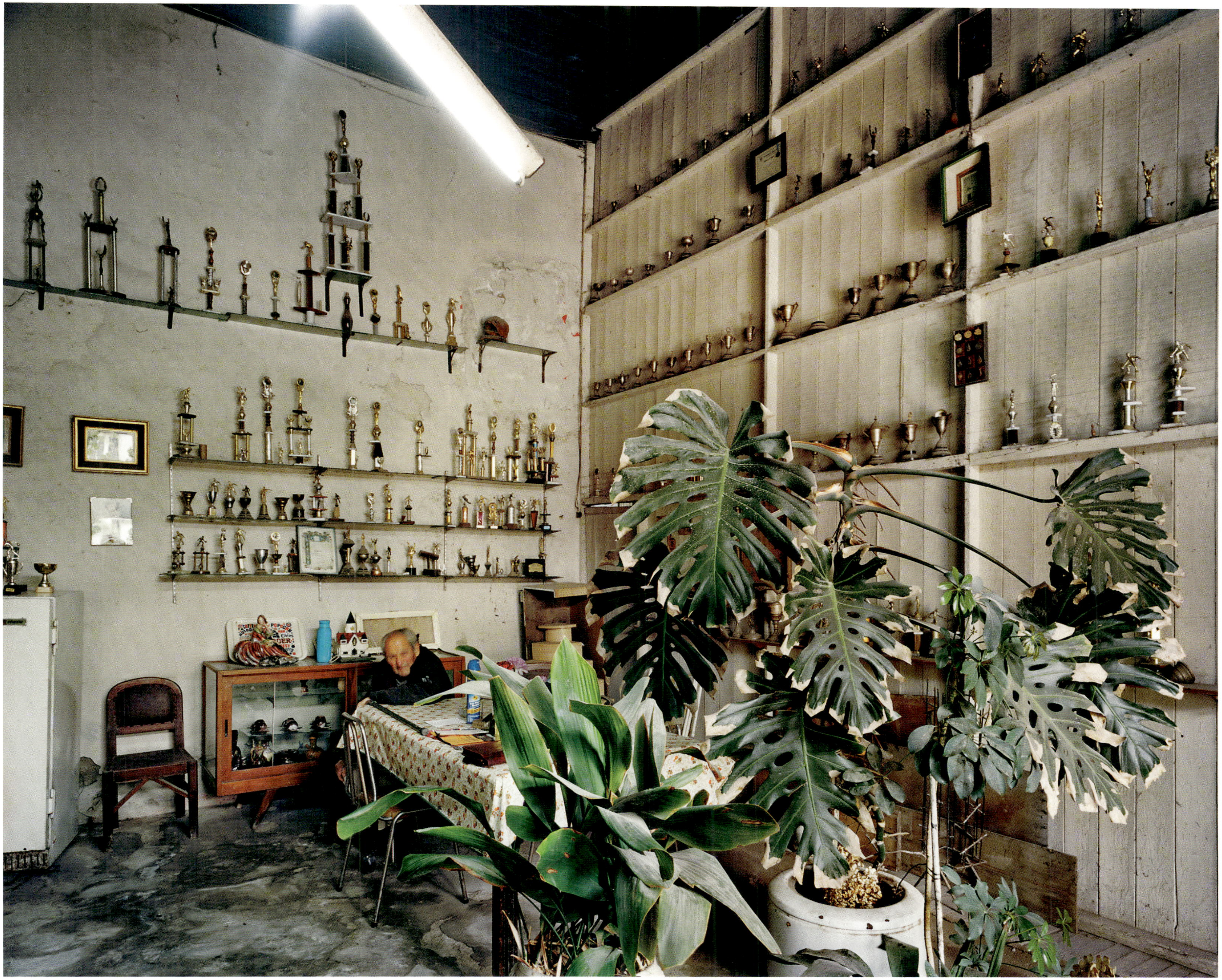

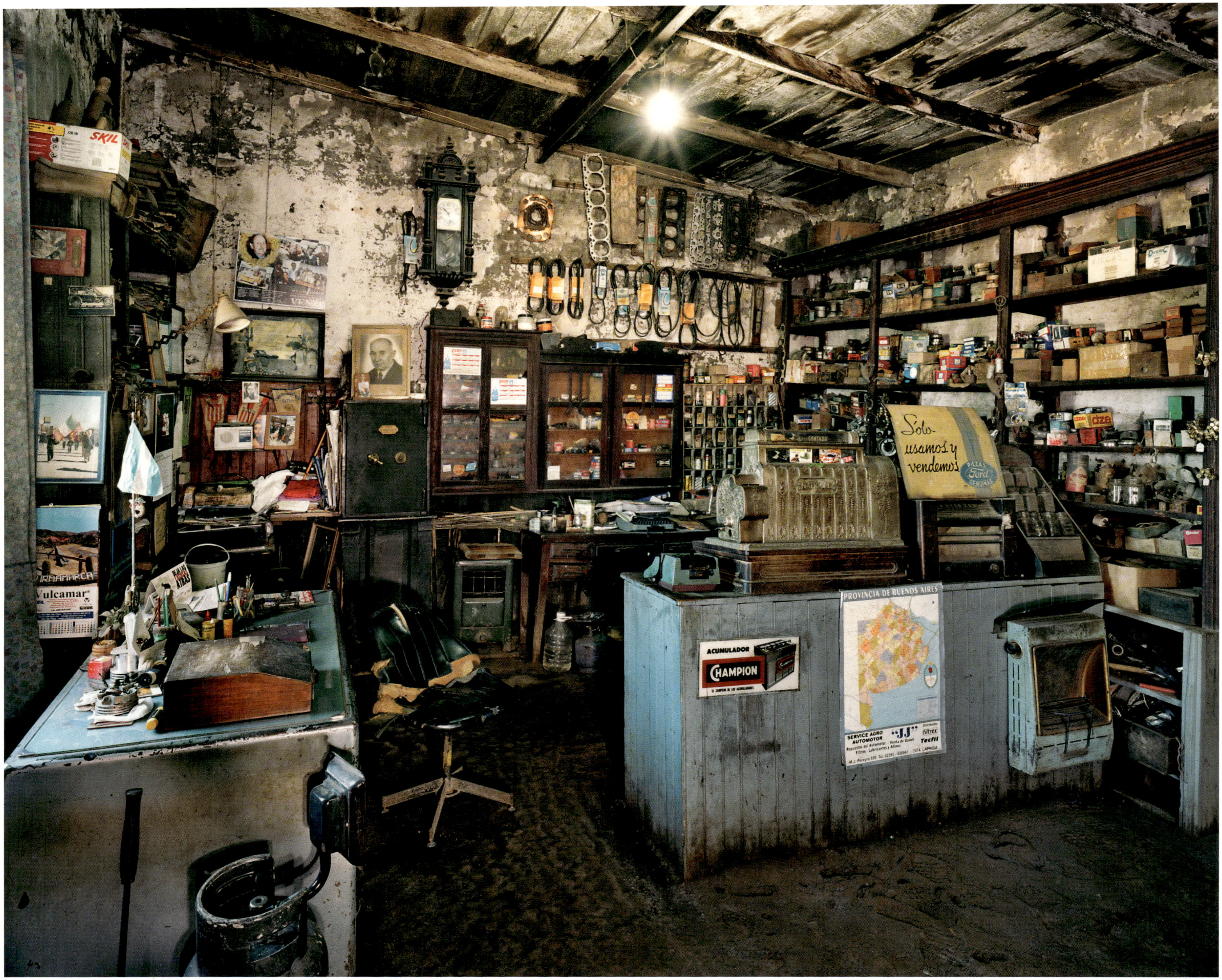
SKIL
Vulcamar
Solo usamos y vendemos
PIEZAS Ford GENUINAS
ACUMULADOR
CHAMPION
PROVINCIA DE BUENOS AIRES
SERVICE AGRO AUTOMOTOR
"JJ"
filtrex
Tecfil

41

Casa Bolognani 2014

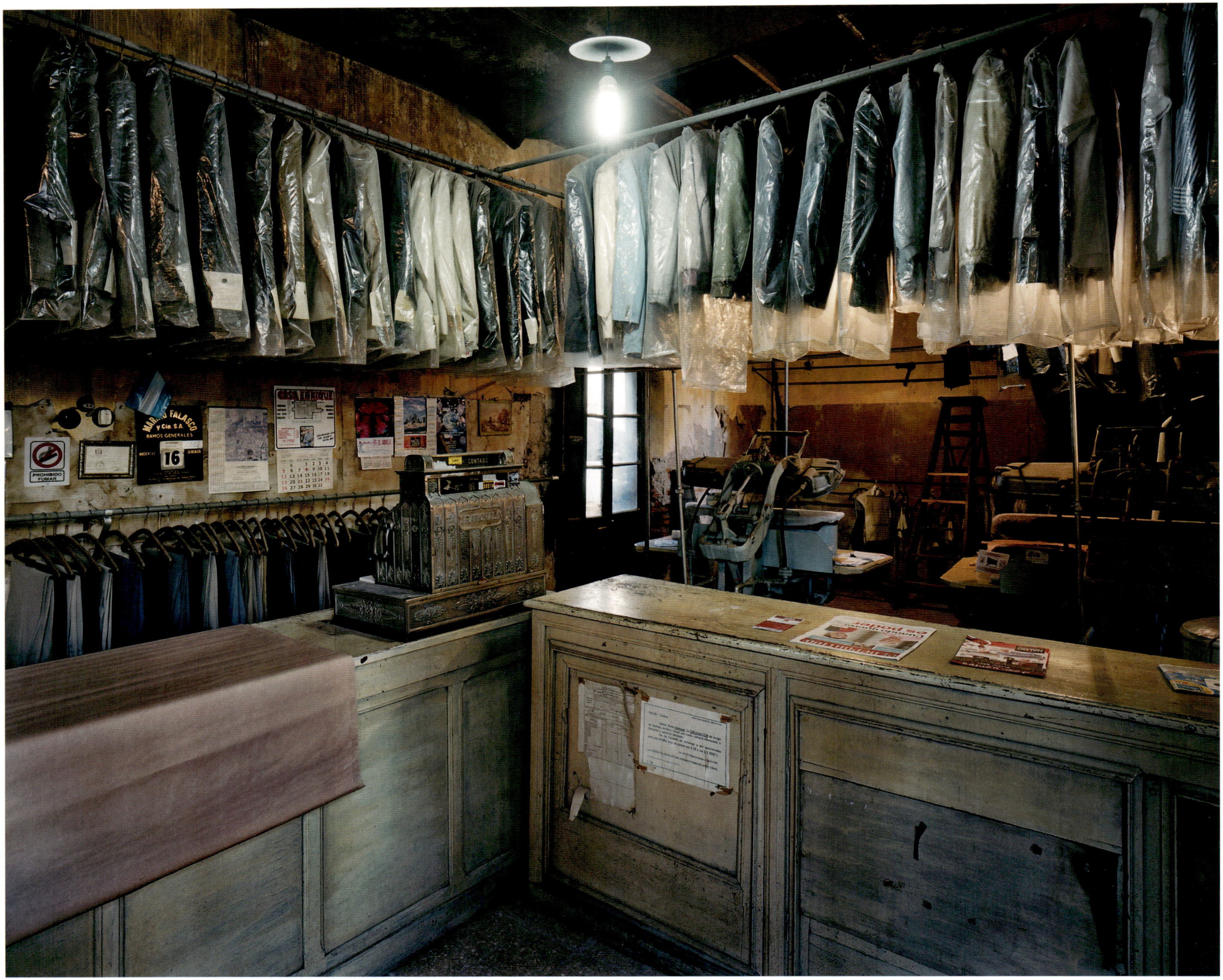
PROHIBIDO
FUMAR
y Cia. S.A.
RAMOS GENERALES
16
CONTADO

43 **Japón Dry Cleaners** 2008

El Ombú Fodder Shop 2008

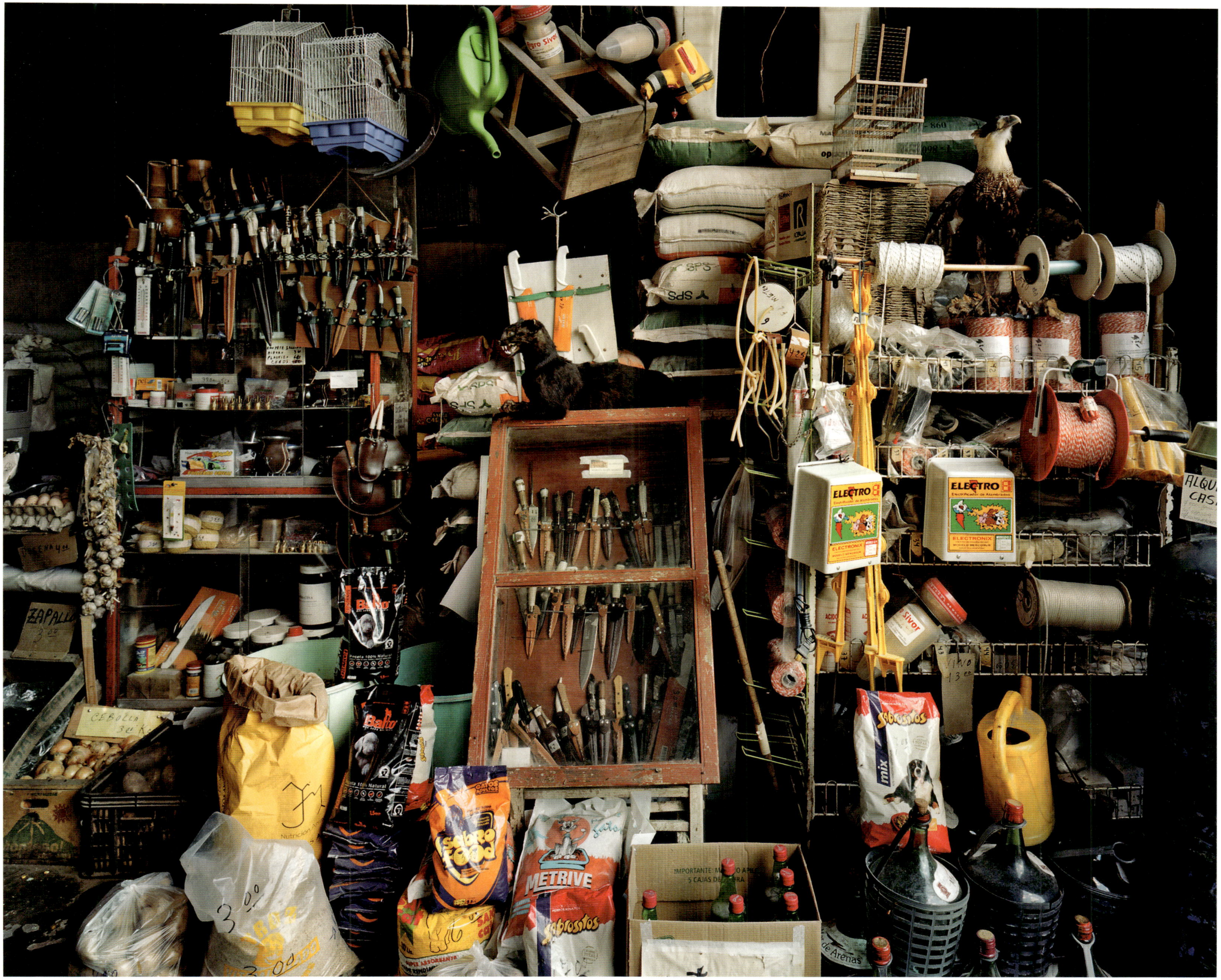
ELECTRO
ELECTRONIX
METRIVE
Sabrositos
mix
Balto
SPS
ZAPALLO
IMPORTANTE

Sol De Mayo General Store 2009

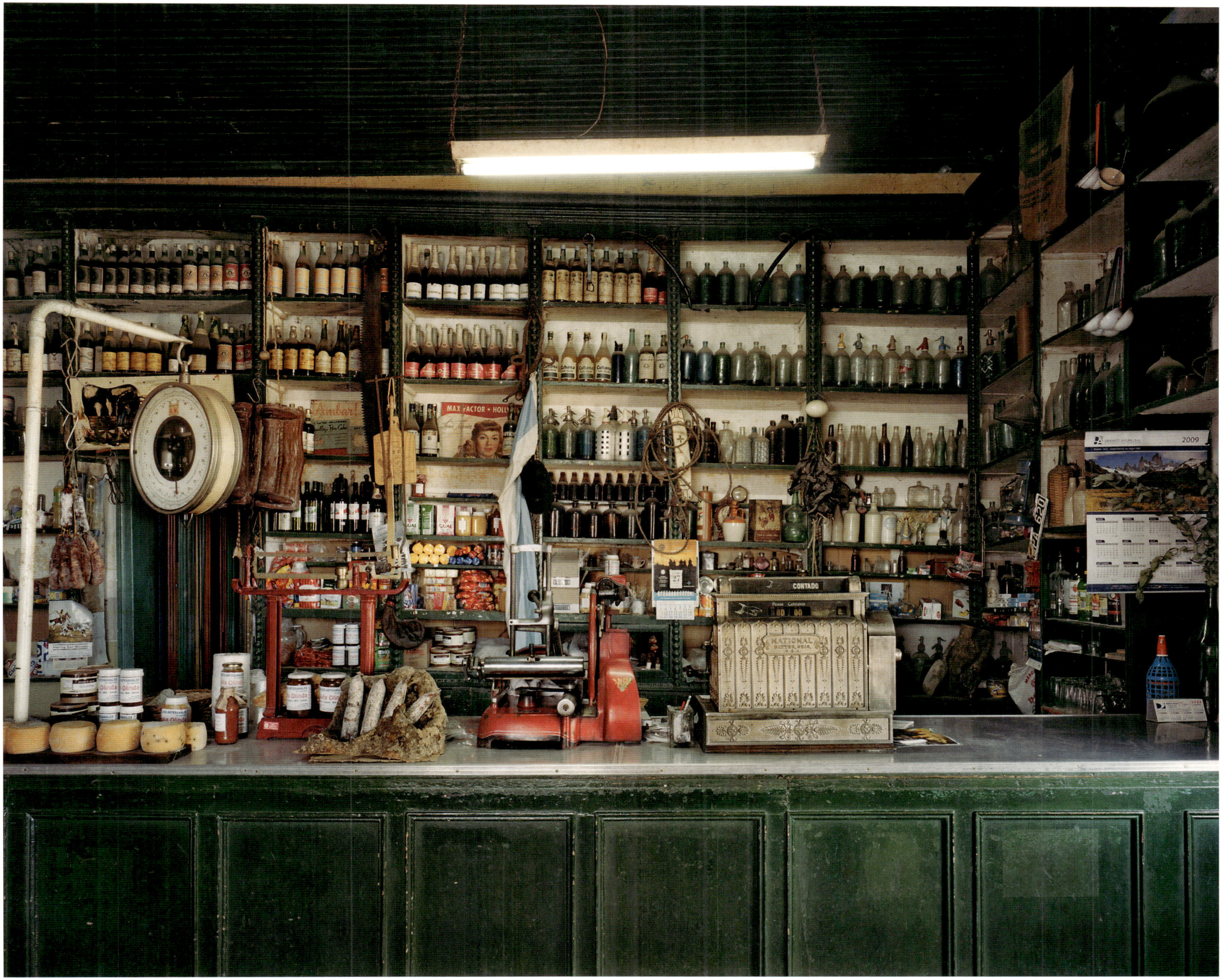
MAX FACTOR · HOLLY
CONTADO
NATIONAL
2009

La Paz General Store 2009

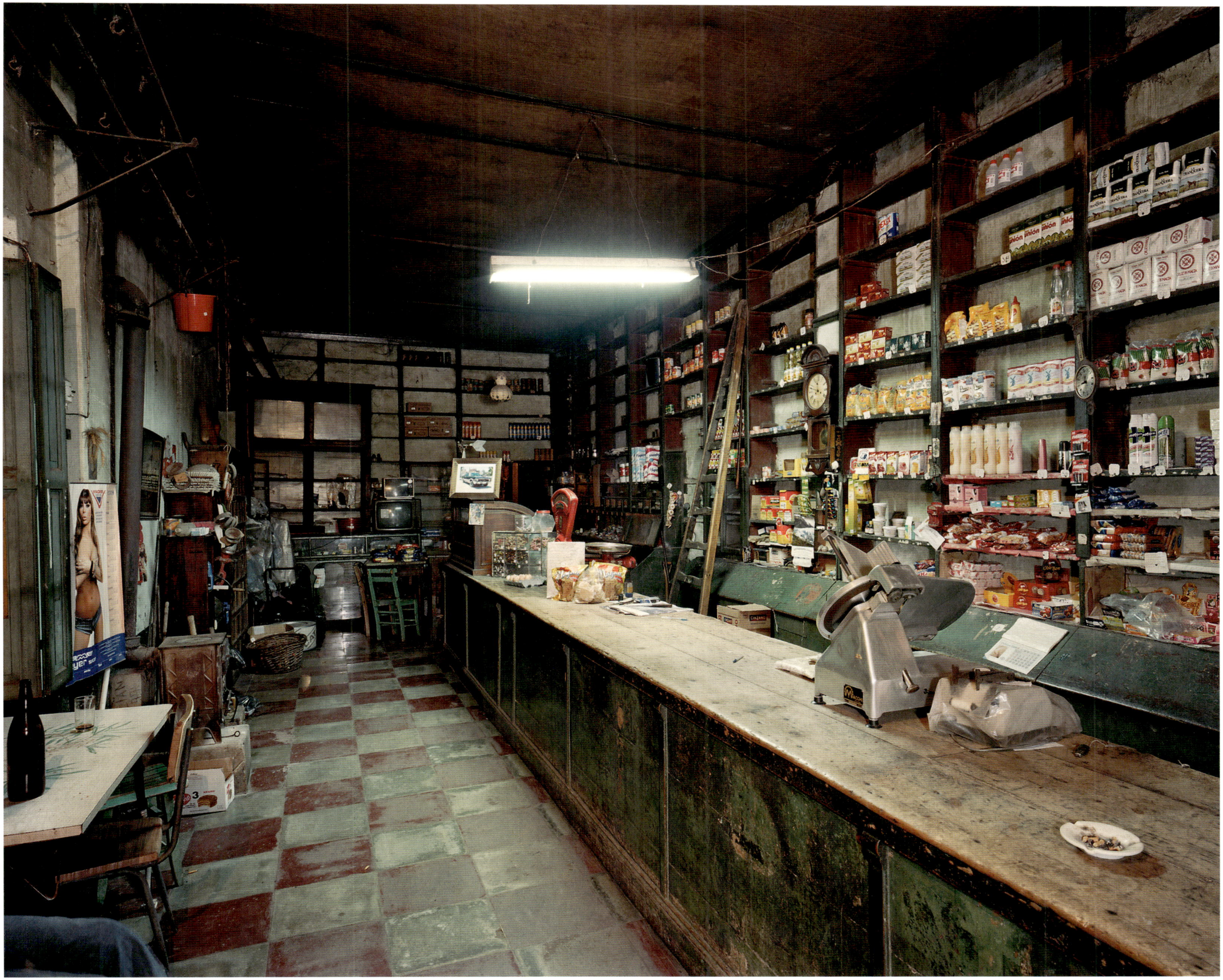

Tala General Store 2010

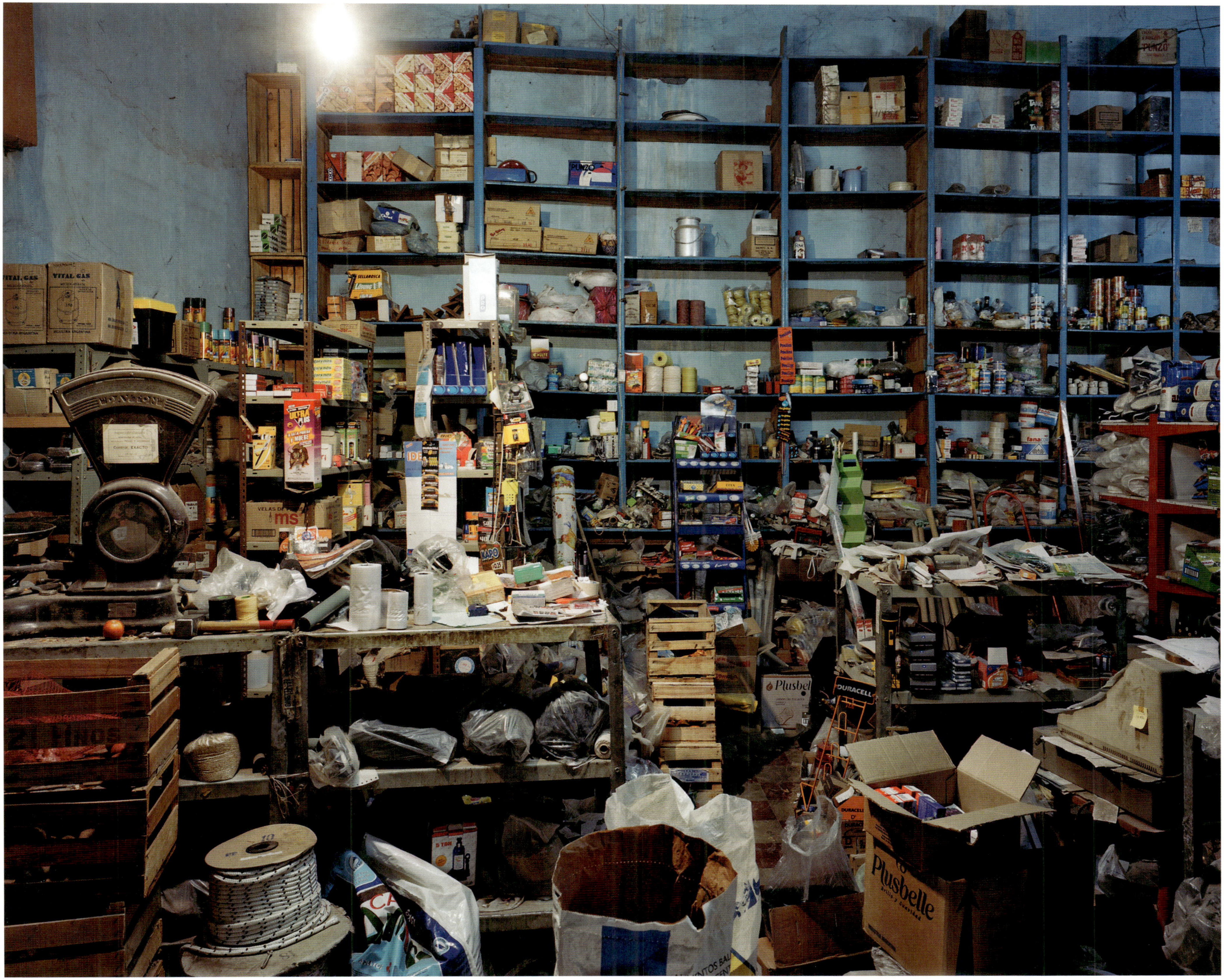
VITAL GAS
PUNZO
ULTRA PLUS
DURACELL
Plusbelle

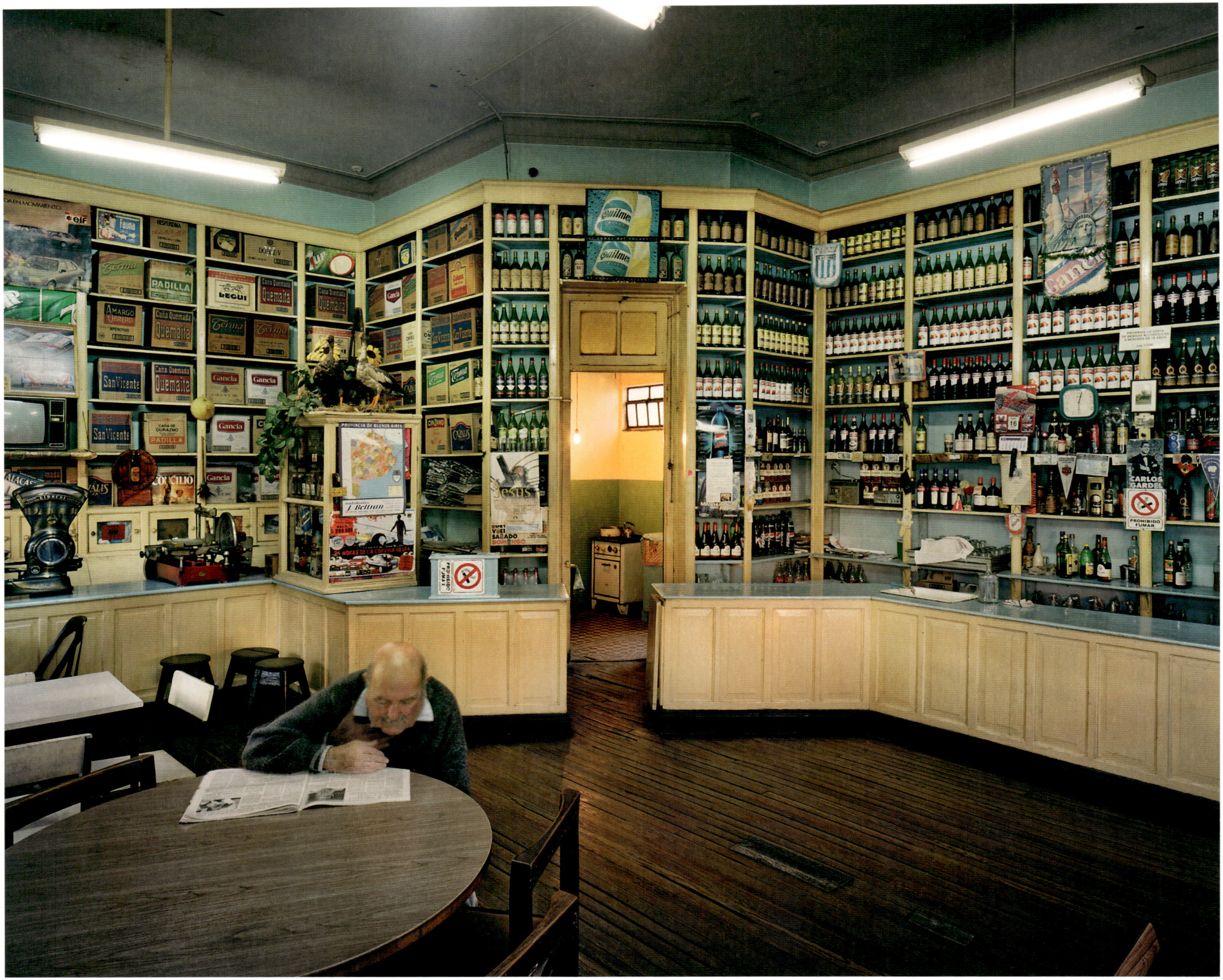

Fauna
Terma
PADILLA
BEGUI
Quemaita
Amargo Obrero
Caña Quemada
San Vicente
Gancia
Quilmes
PROVINCIA DE BUENOS AIRES
J. Beltran
Jesus
24 HORAS DE LA CORVINA NEGRA
CARLOS GARDEL
PROHIBIDO FUMAR

53 **Bar Firpo** 2013

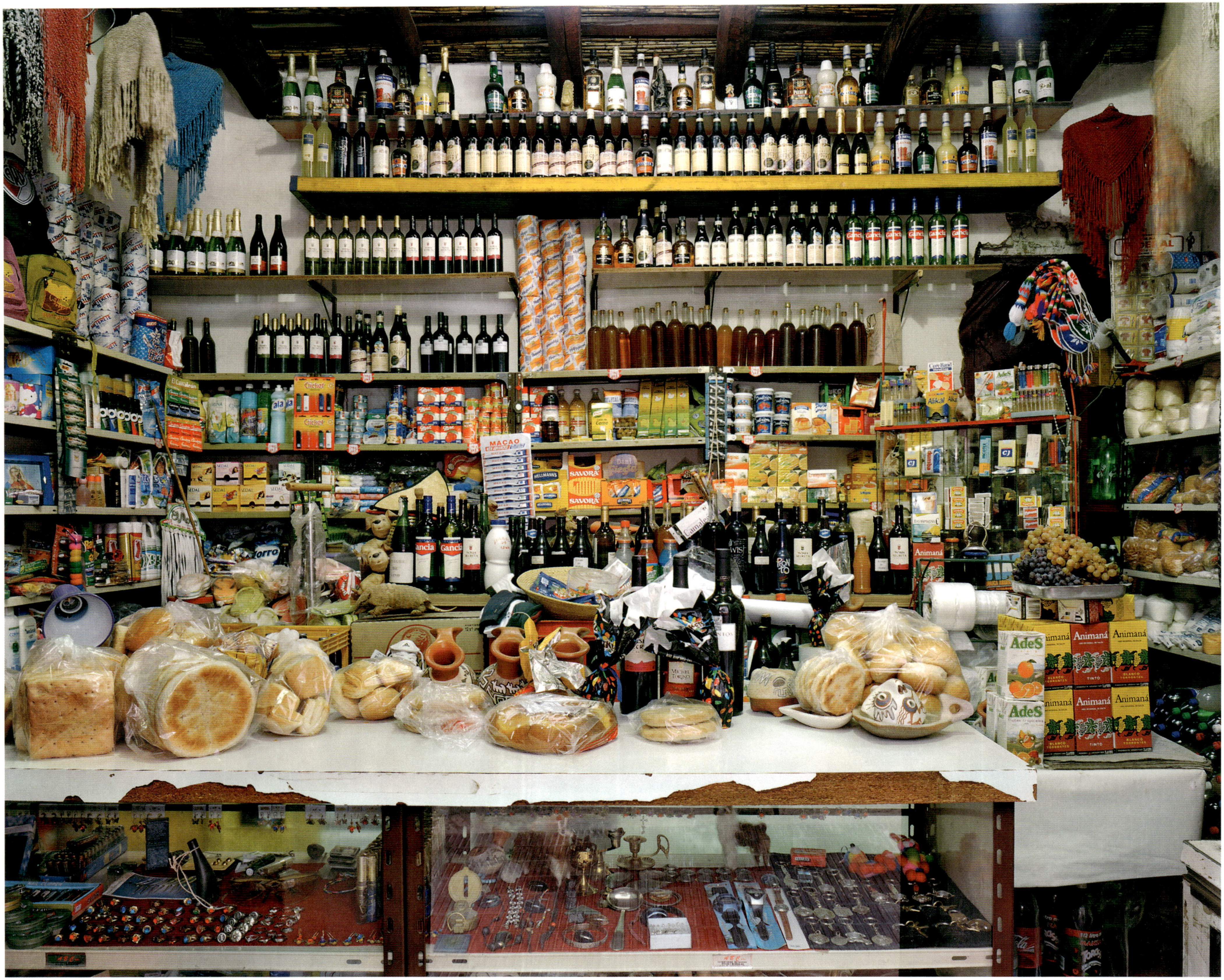
Gancia
SAVORA
AdeS
Animaná
TINTO

55 **Cardón Kiosk** 2006

Campodónico General Store 2011 56

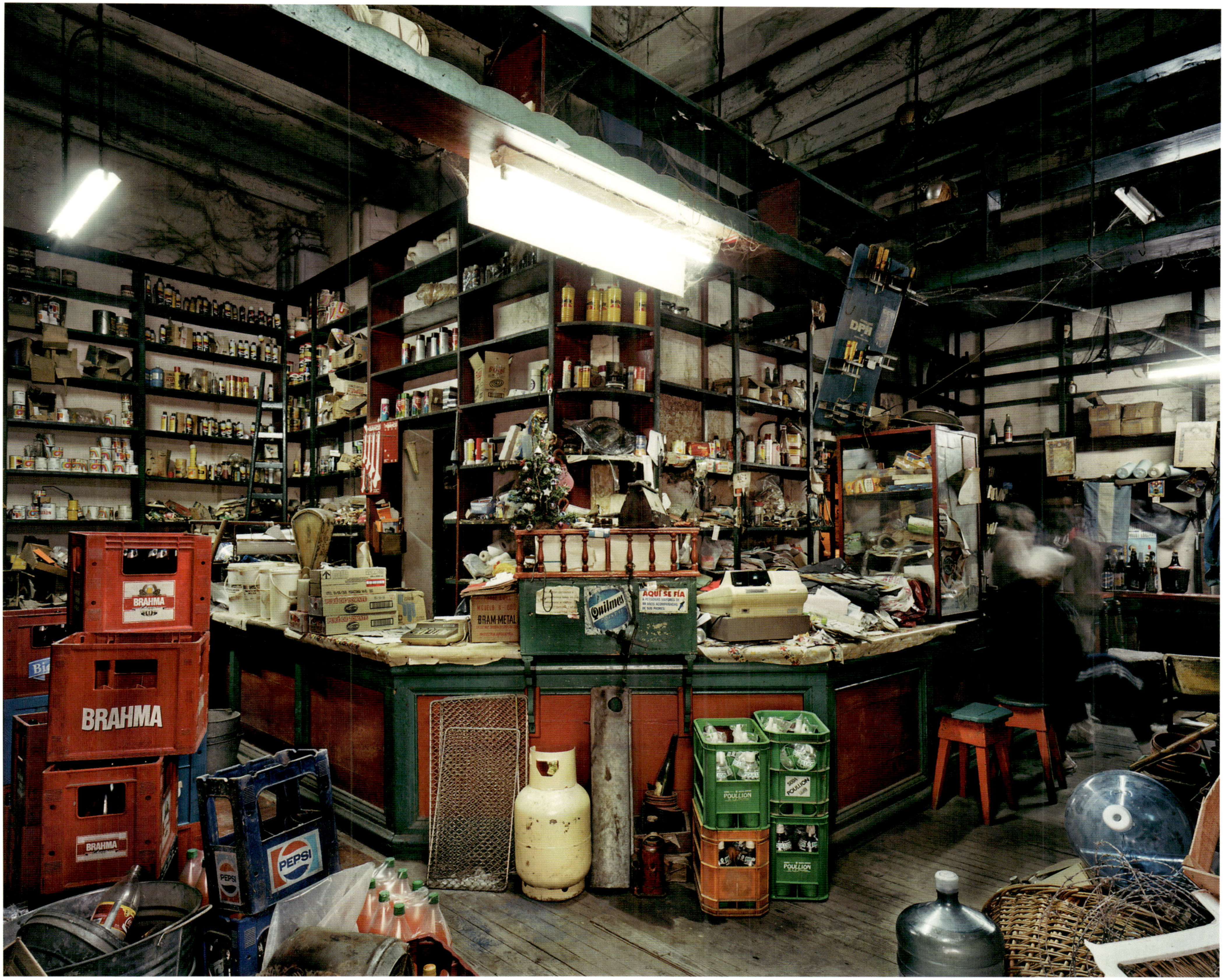

BRAHMA
BRAHMA
BRAHMA
PEPSI
PEPSI
Quilmes
AQUÍ SE FÍA
BRAM-METAL
POULLION

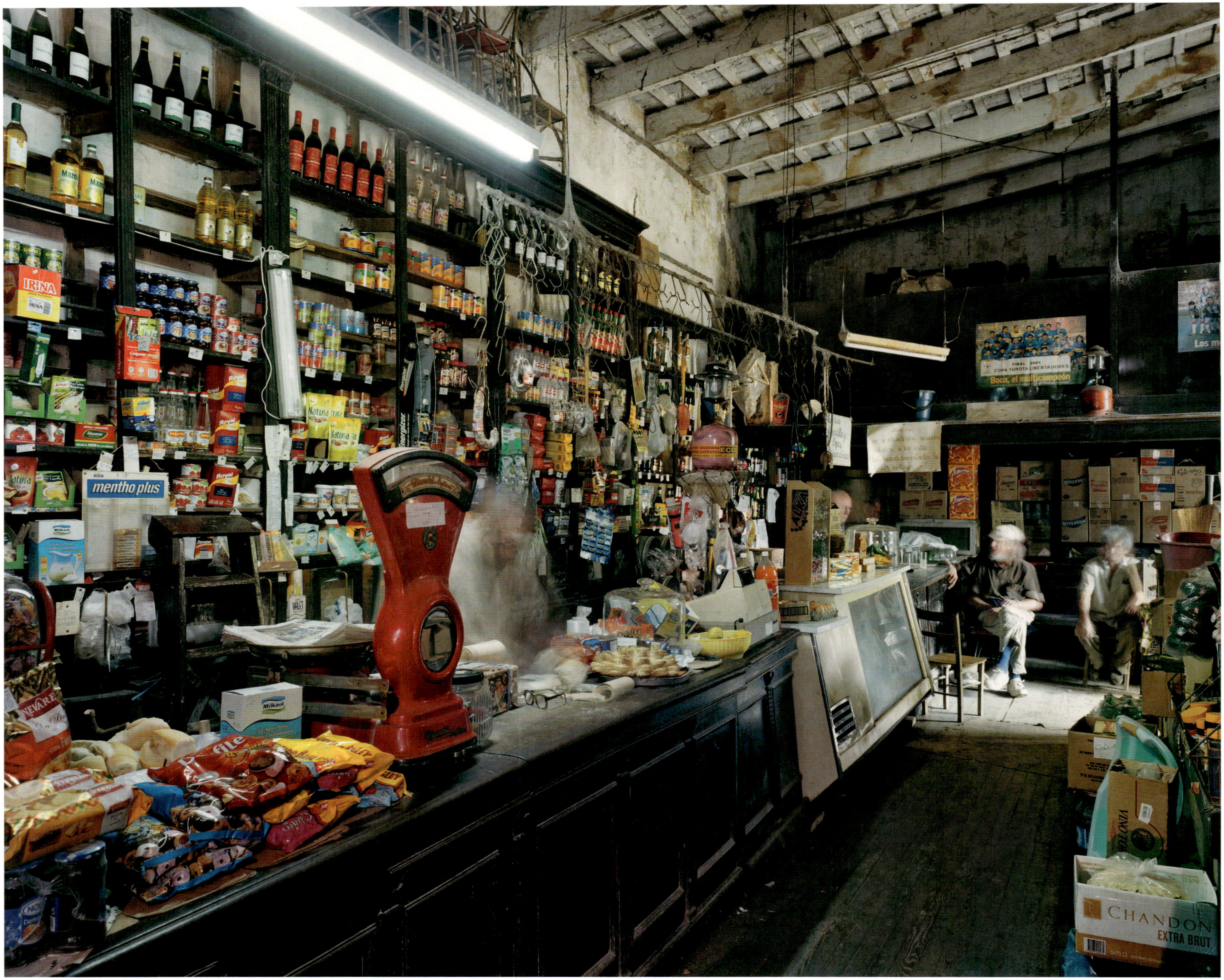

IRINA
mentho plus
Milkaut
Natura
Royal
FINAL 2001
COPA TOYOTA LIBERTADORES
Boca, el multicampeón
CHANDON
EXTRA BRUT

59 **13 Hermanos General Store** 2013

Adelfa's Market 2009

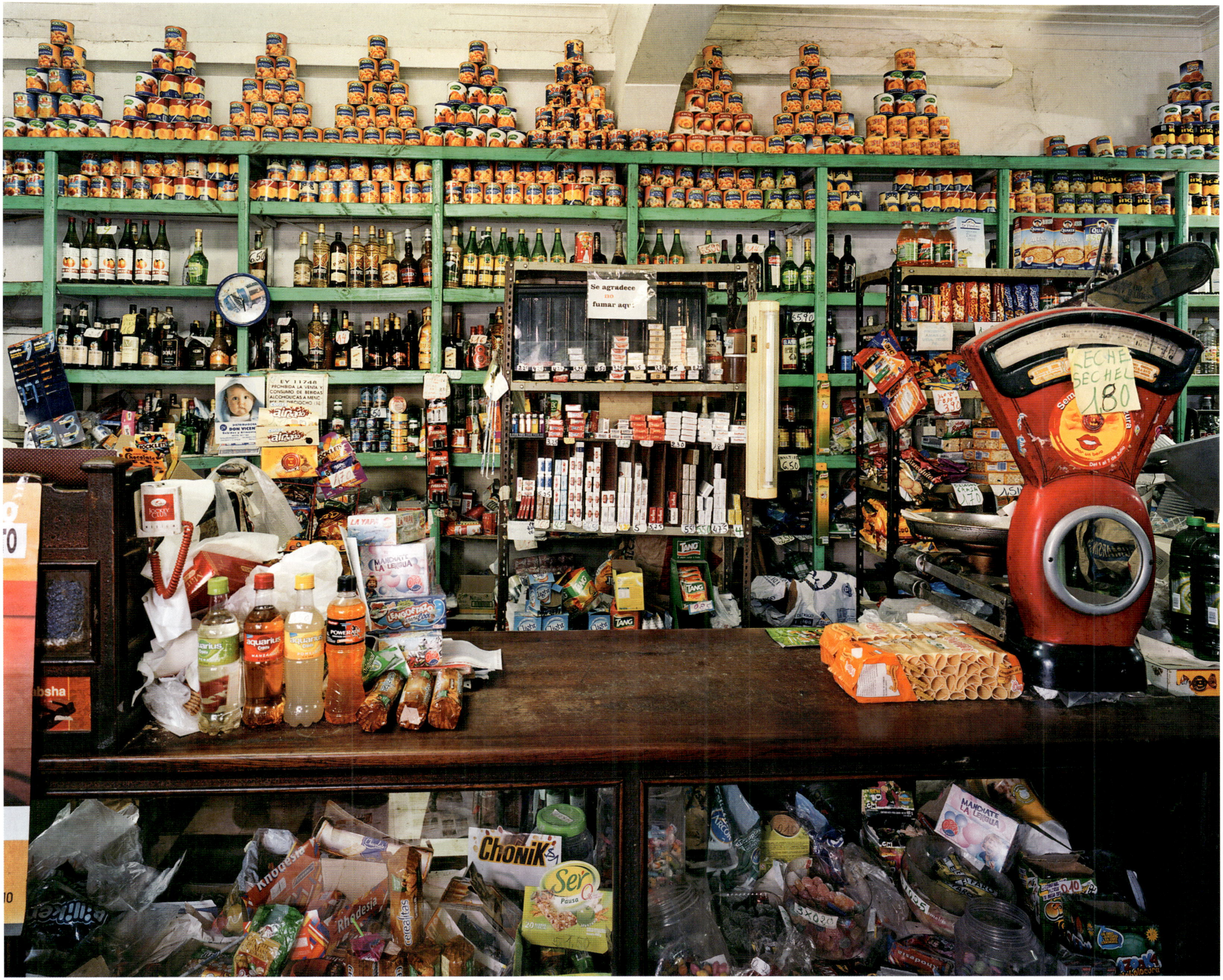
Se agradece
no
fumar aquí
LECHE
SECHEL
180
TANG
aquarius
Chonik's
Ser
Pausa
Rhodesia
cerealitas

Trecu Pharmacy 2013

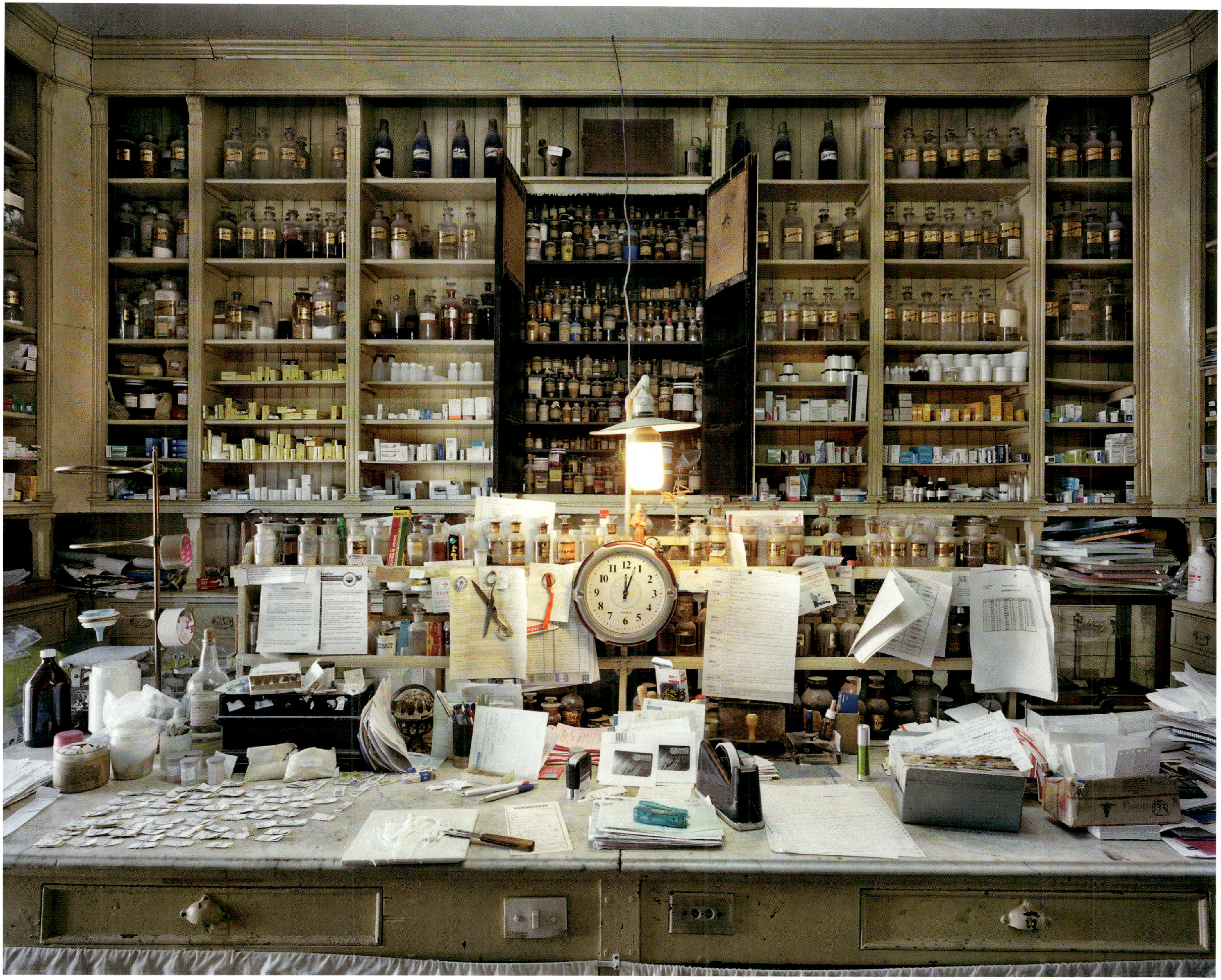

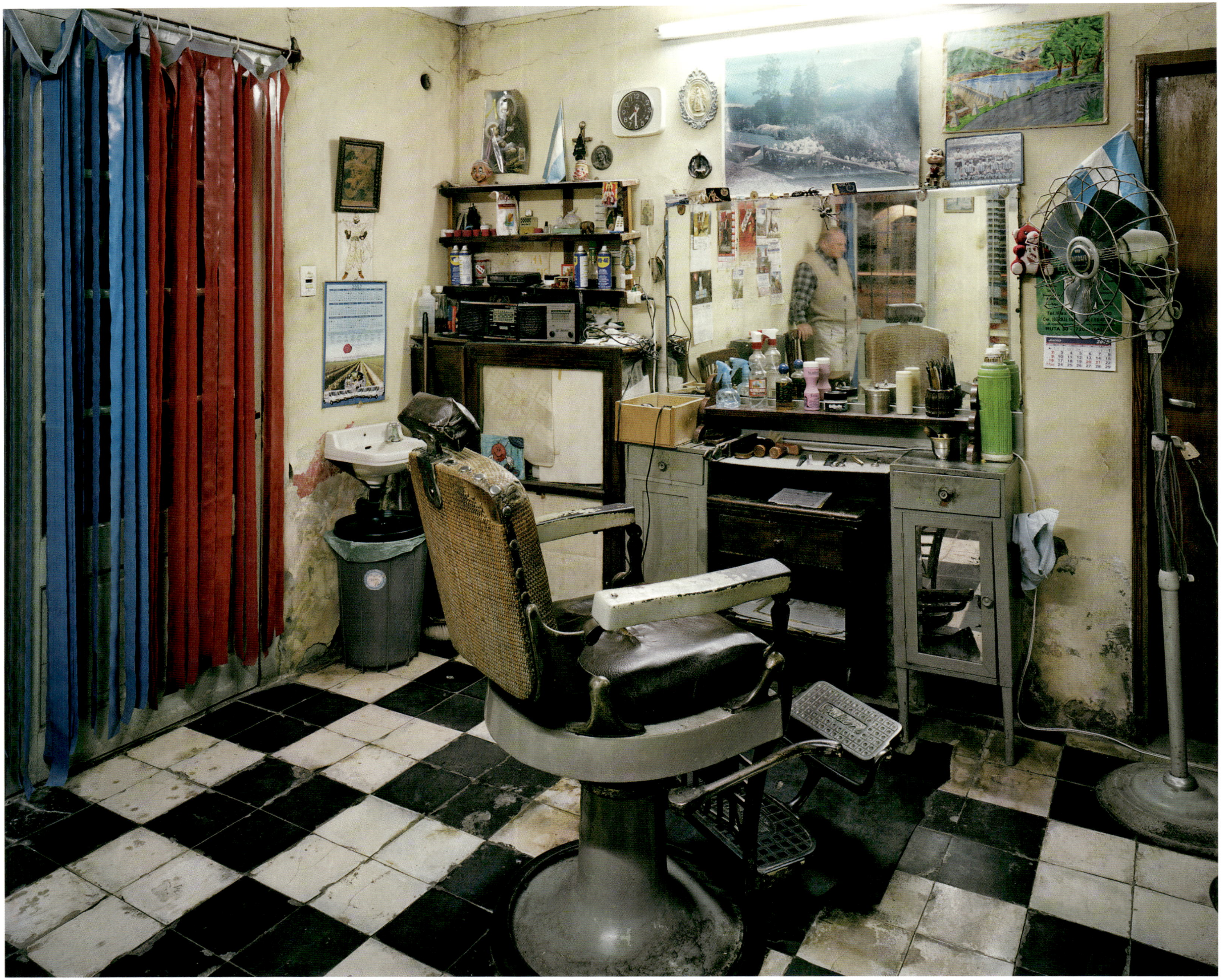

65 **Town Barber** 2013

“El 91” Butcher Shop 2006

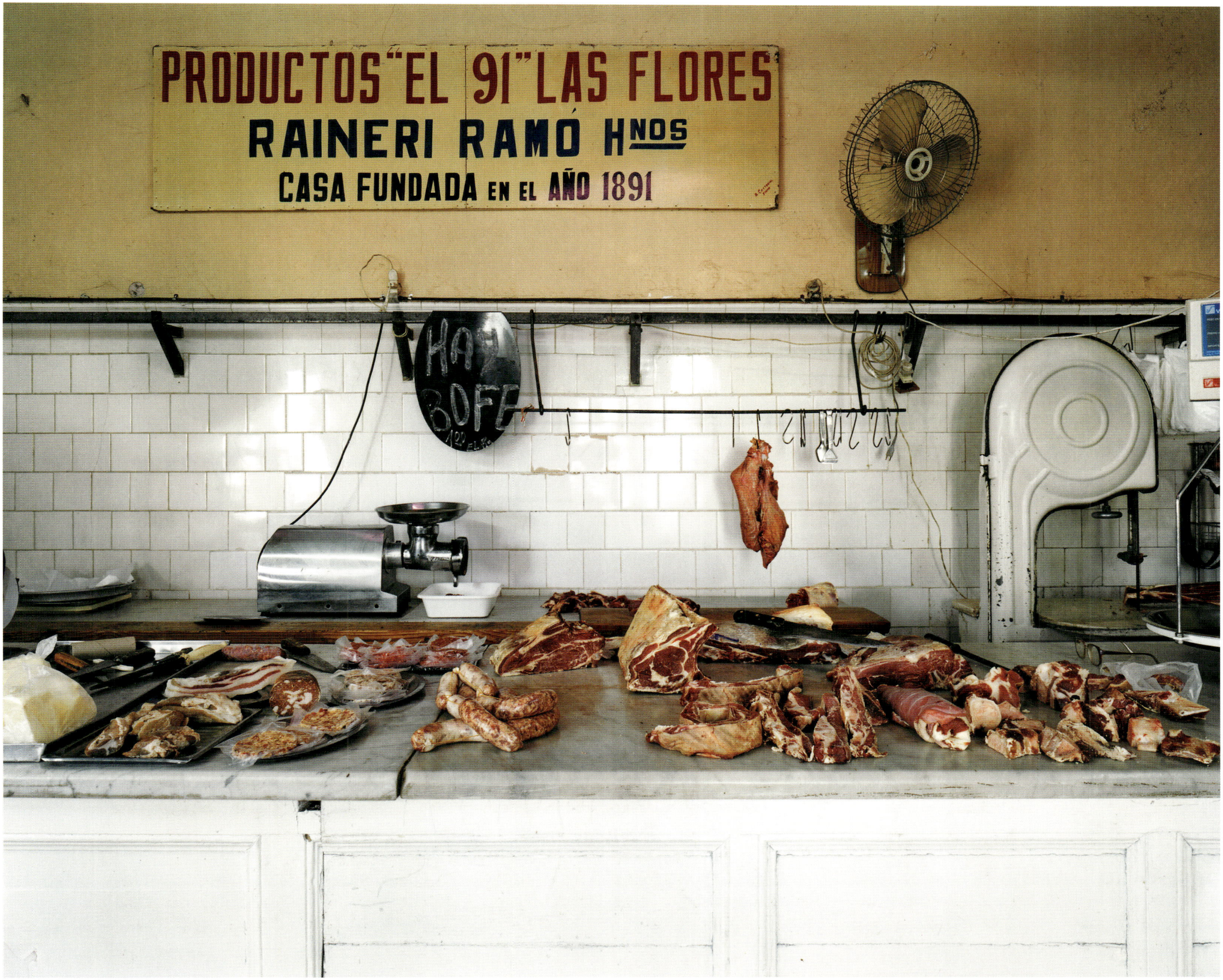
PRODUCTOS "EL 91" LAS FLORES
RAINERI RAMÓ Hnos
CASA FUNDADA EN EL AÑO 1891
HAY
BOFE

Los Agapantos Pork Products 2014 68

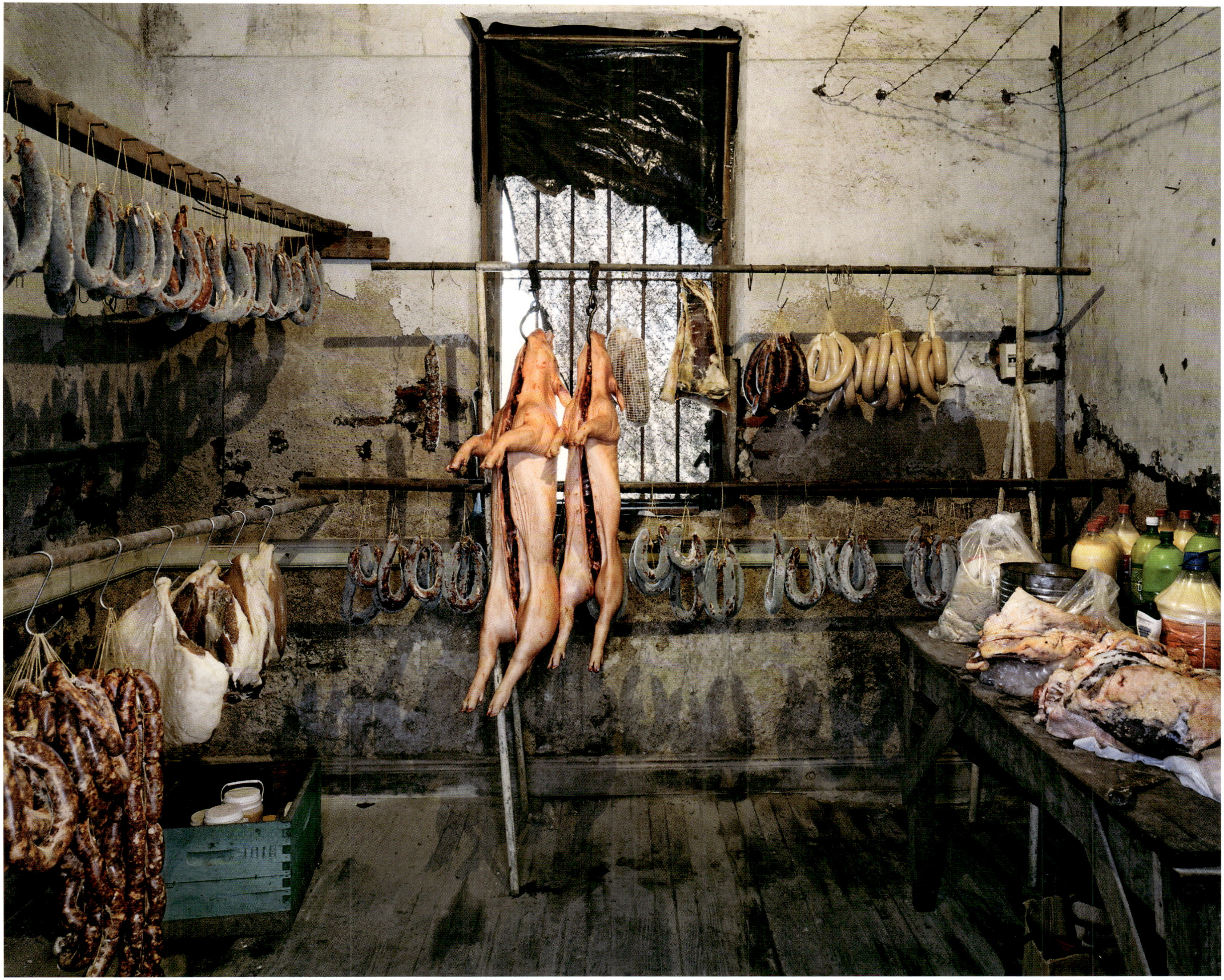

Sheep Rennets 2006

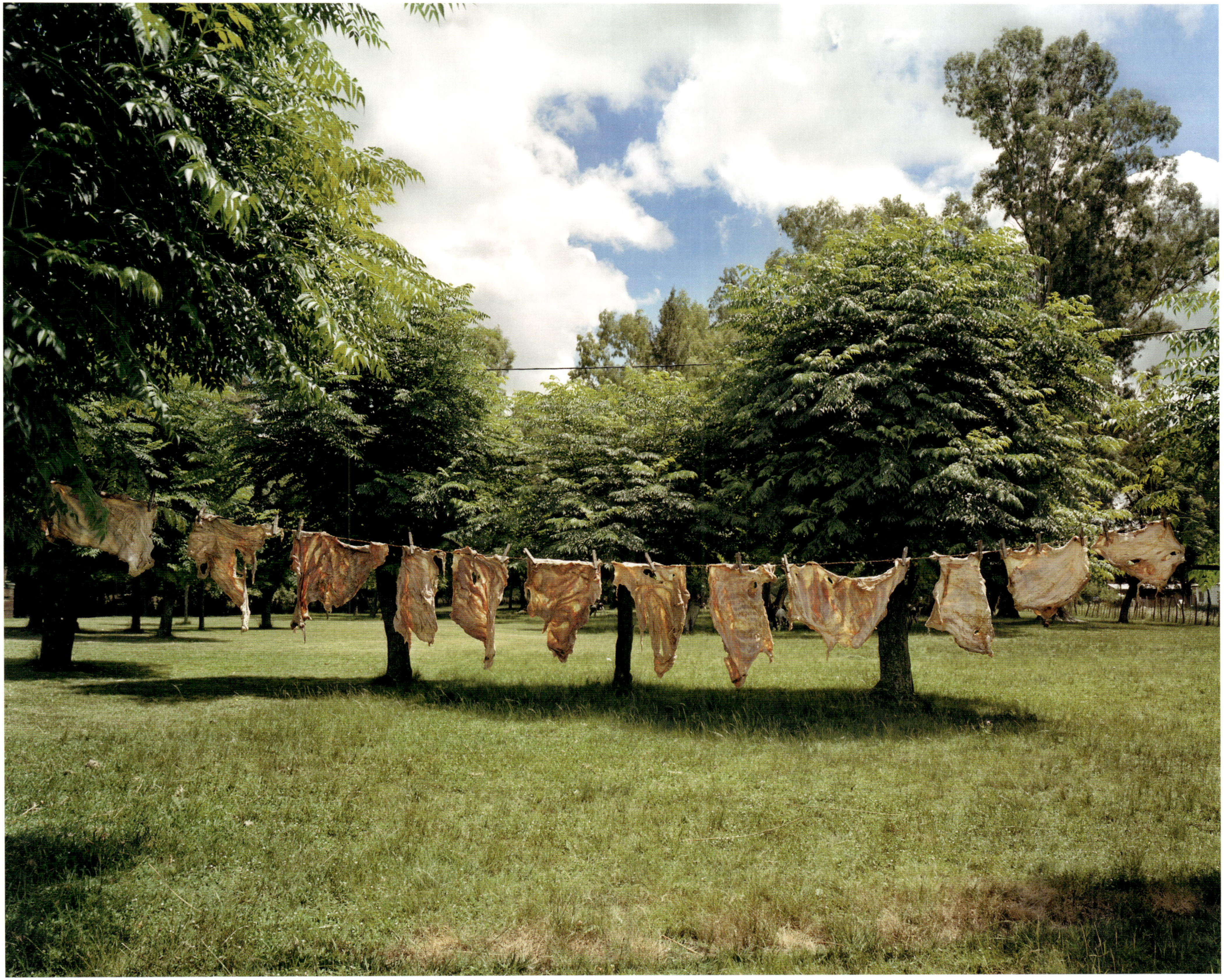

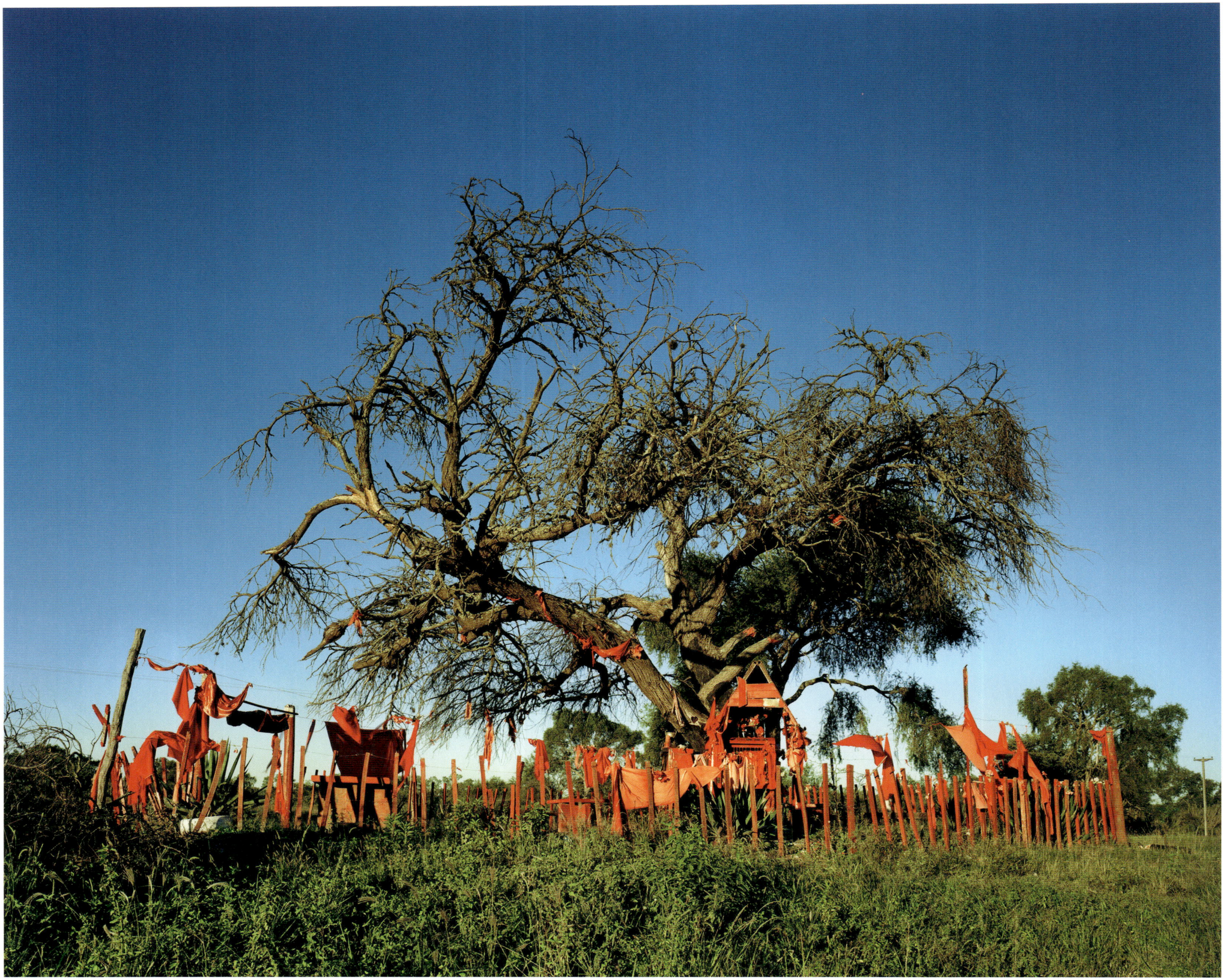

73 **Gauchito Gil Shrine, Route 34** 2006

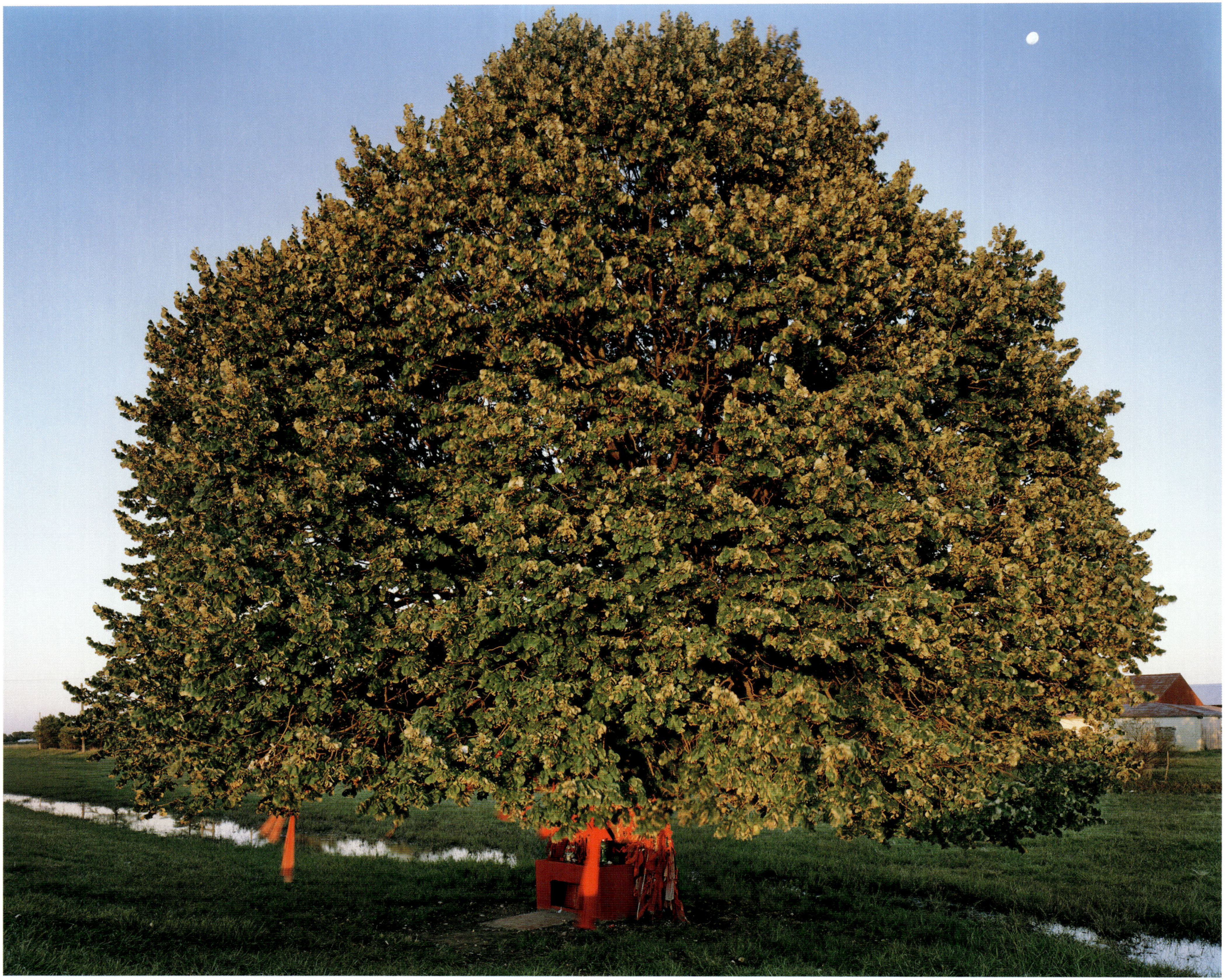

75 **Gauchito Gil Shrine / Linden Tree** 2005

Armadillo Shells 2007

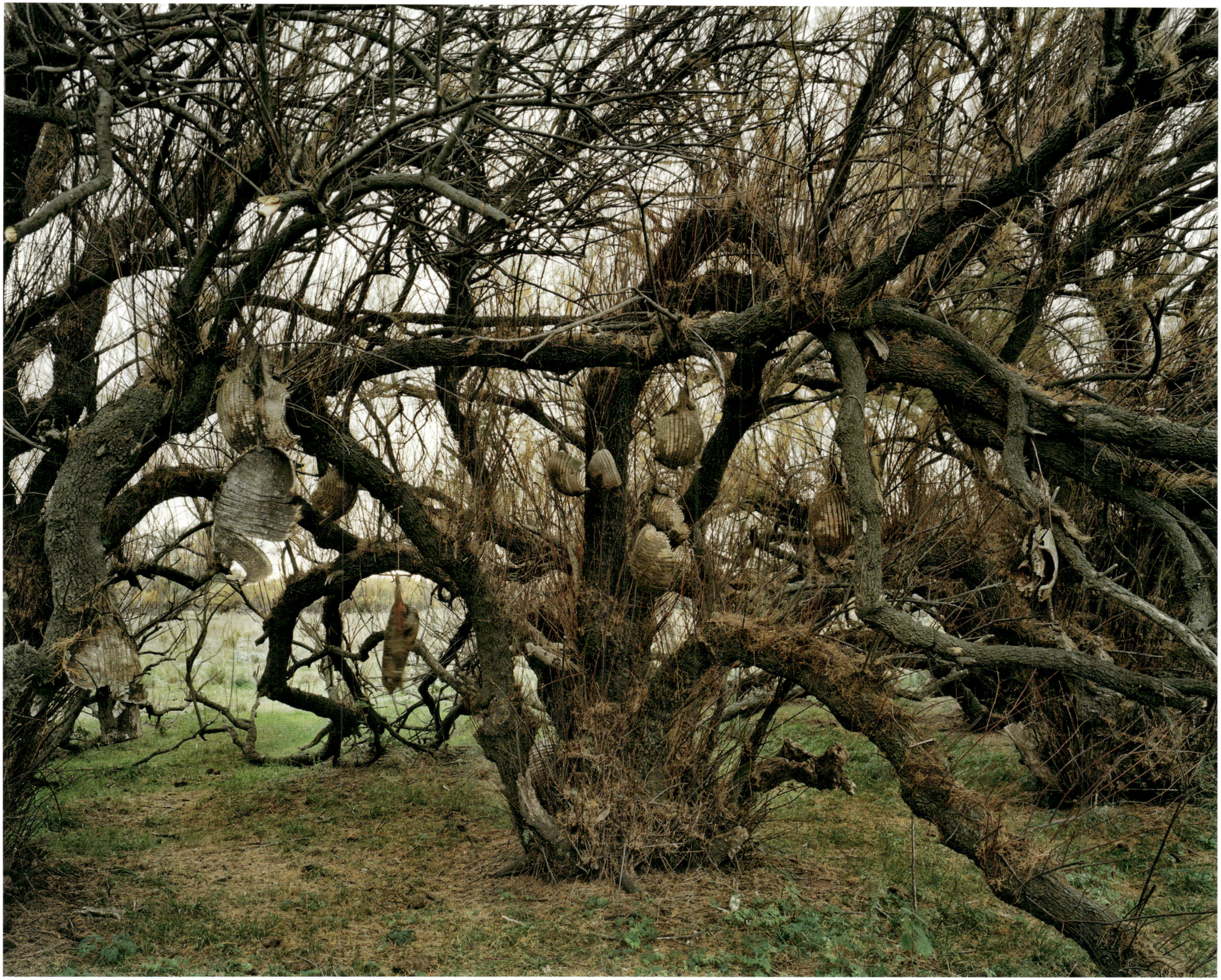

Gauchito Gil Shrine, Route 51 2006

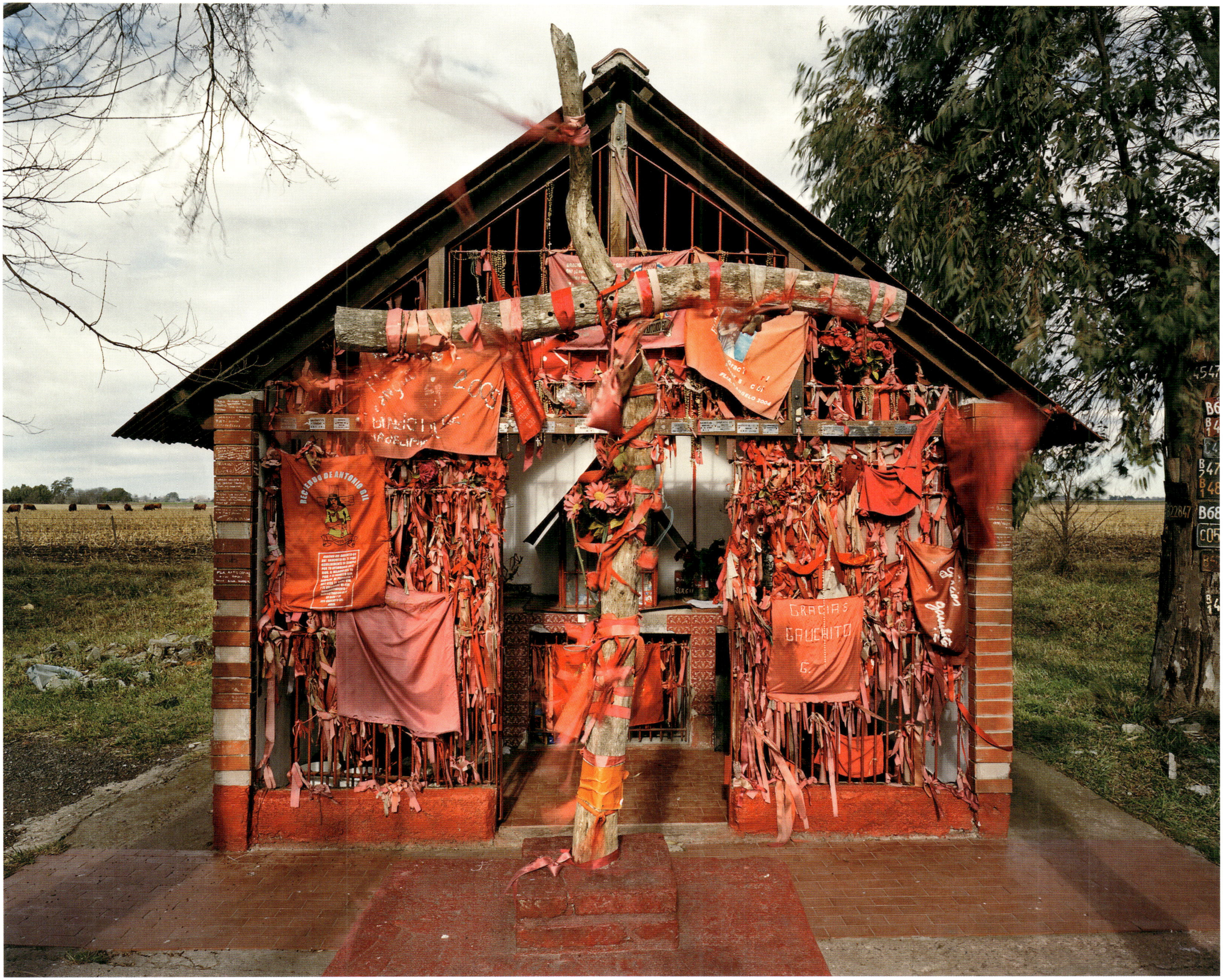
GRACIAS
GAUCHITO
G.

Gauchito Gil Museum 2006

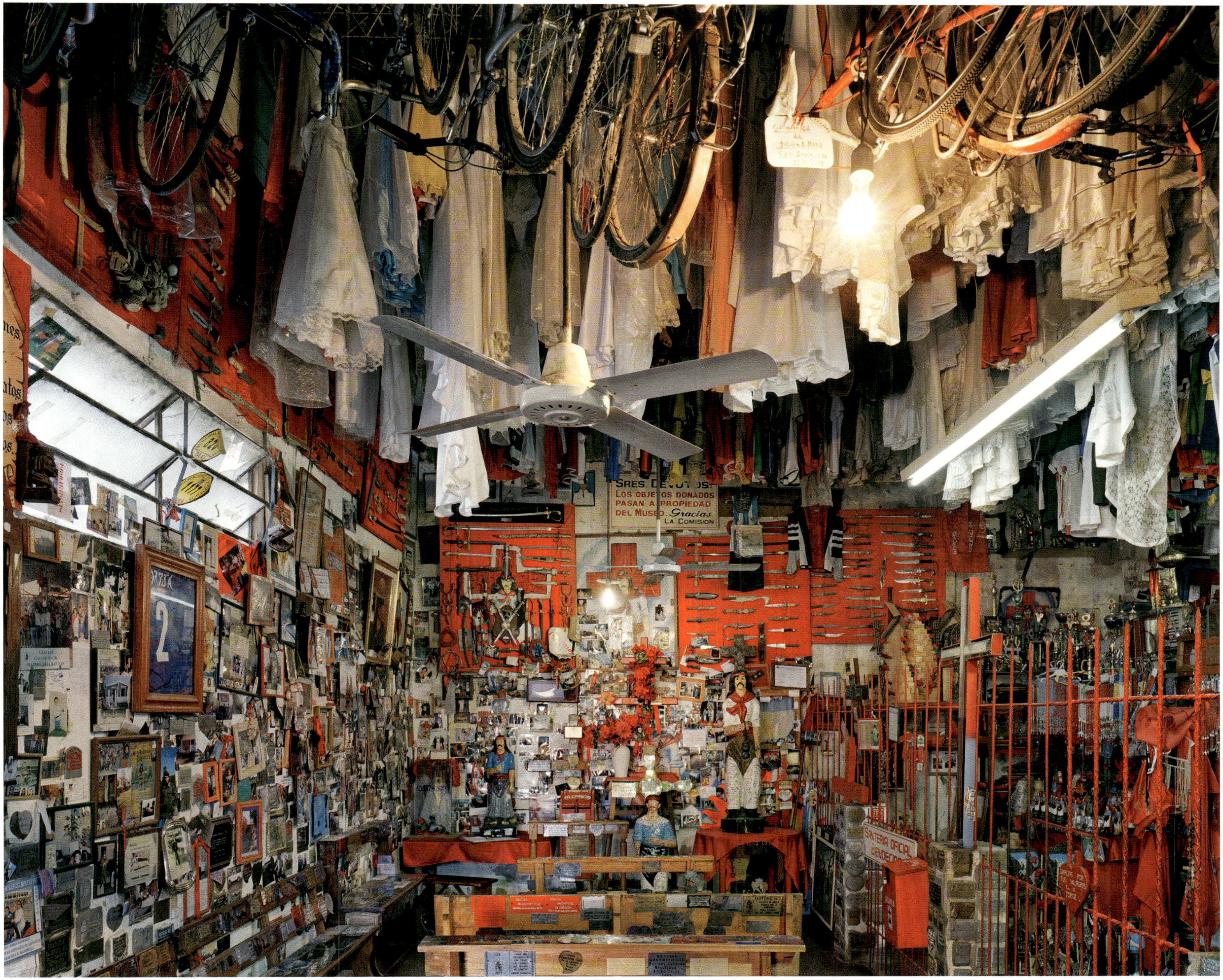
SRES. DEVOTOS:
LOS OBJETOS DONADOS
PASAN A PROPIEDAD
DEL MUSEO. Gracias.
LA COMISION

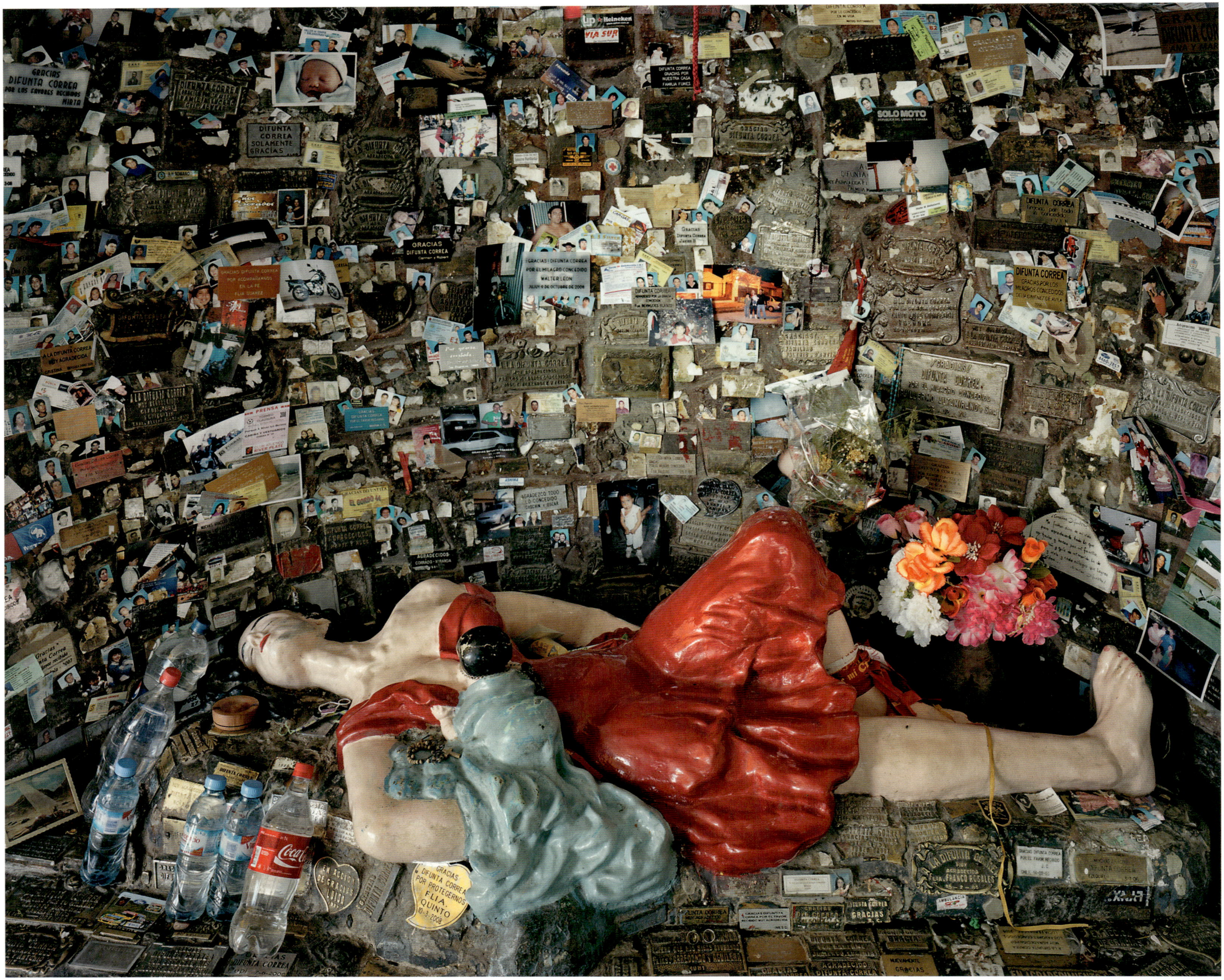

DIFUNTA CORREA
SOLAMENTE
GRACIAS
SOLO MOTO
Heineken
VIA SUR
GRACIAS
DIFUNTA CORREA
Coca-Cola

83 **Difunta Correa Hermit** 2010

Difunta Correa Shrine 2010

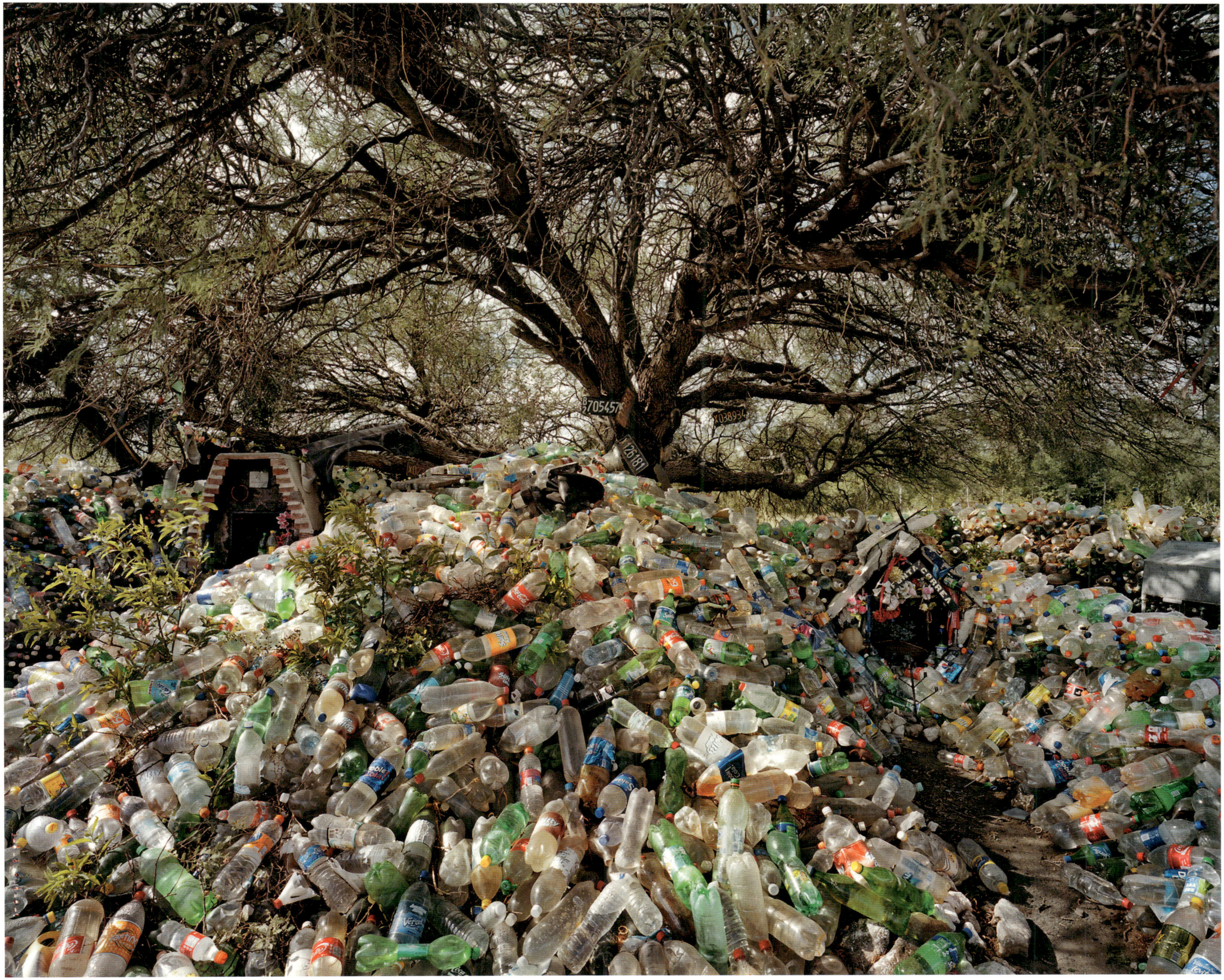

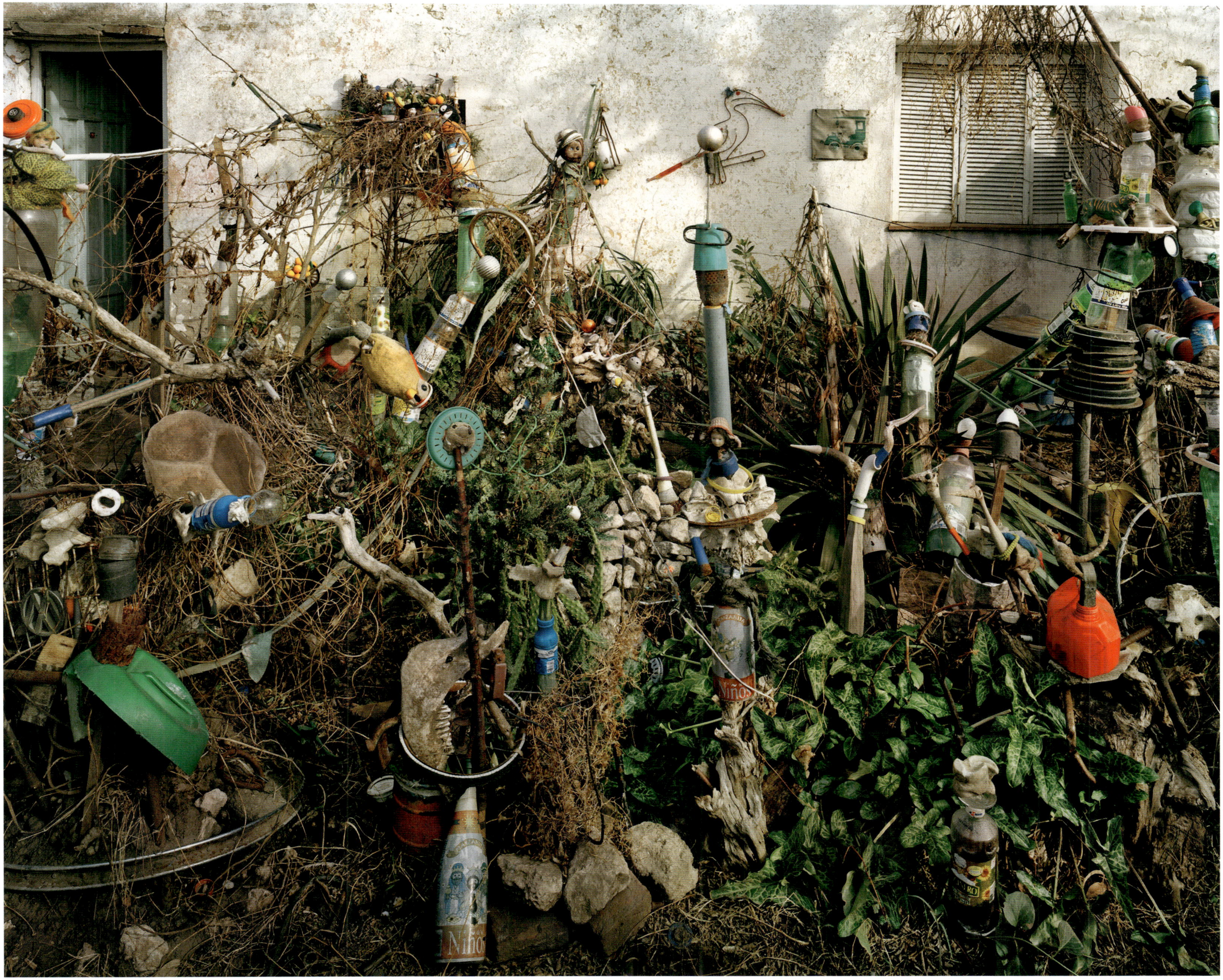
Niños
Niños

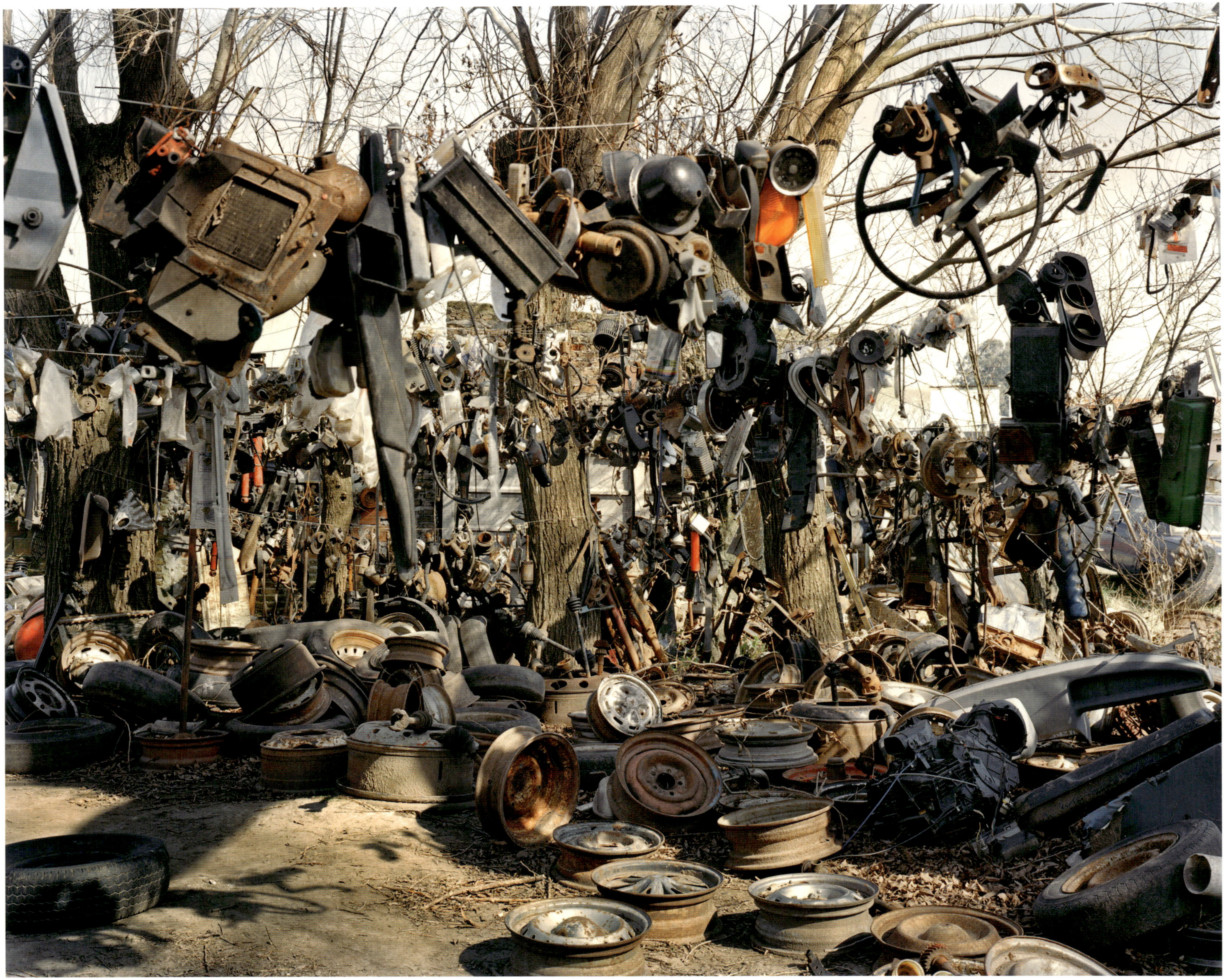

89 **Car Parts** 2007

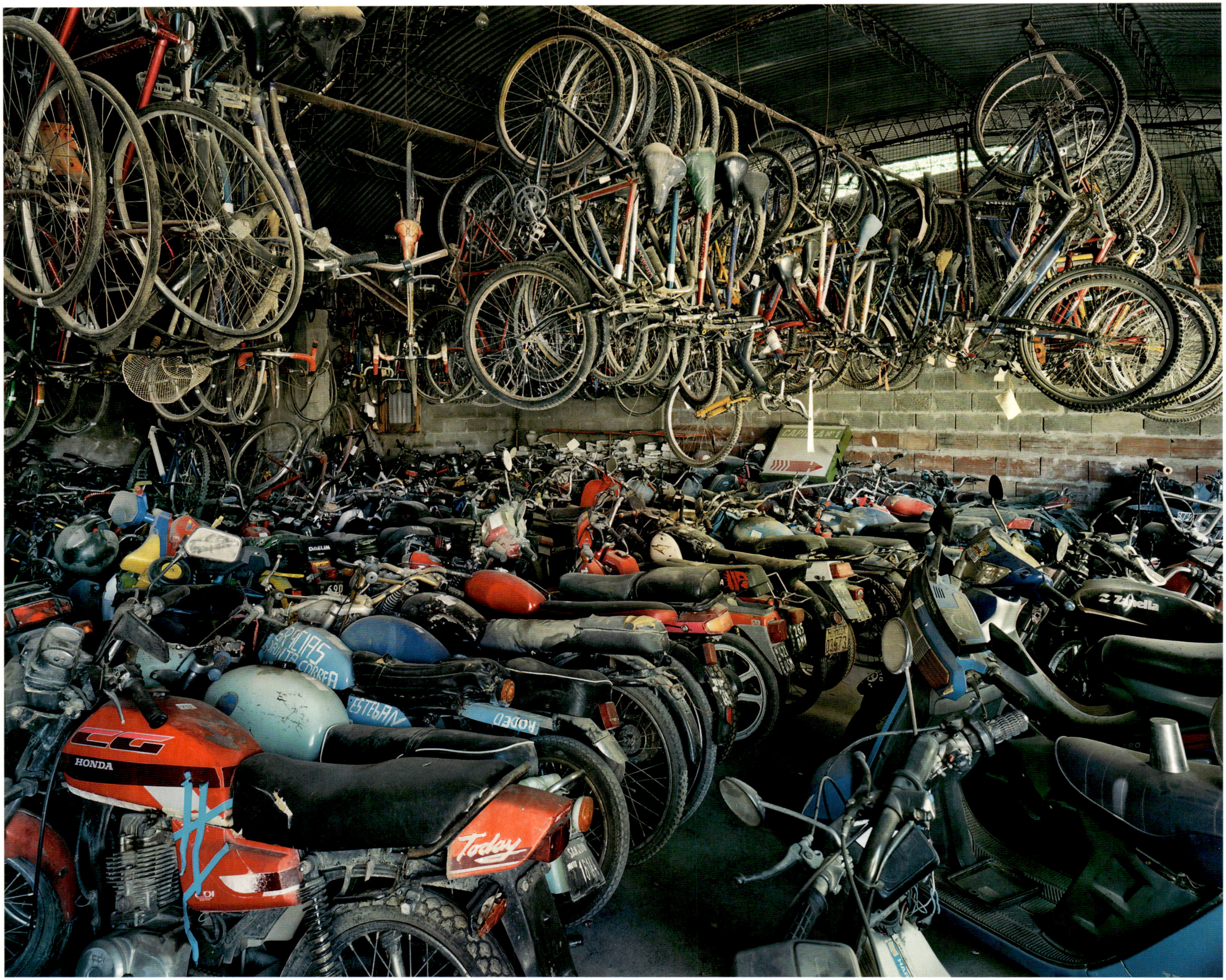
HONDA
Today

91

Difunta Correa Hangar 2010

"El Beto" 2013

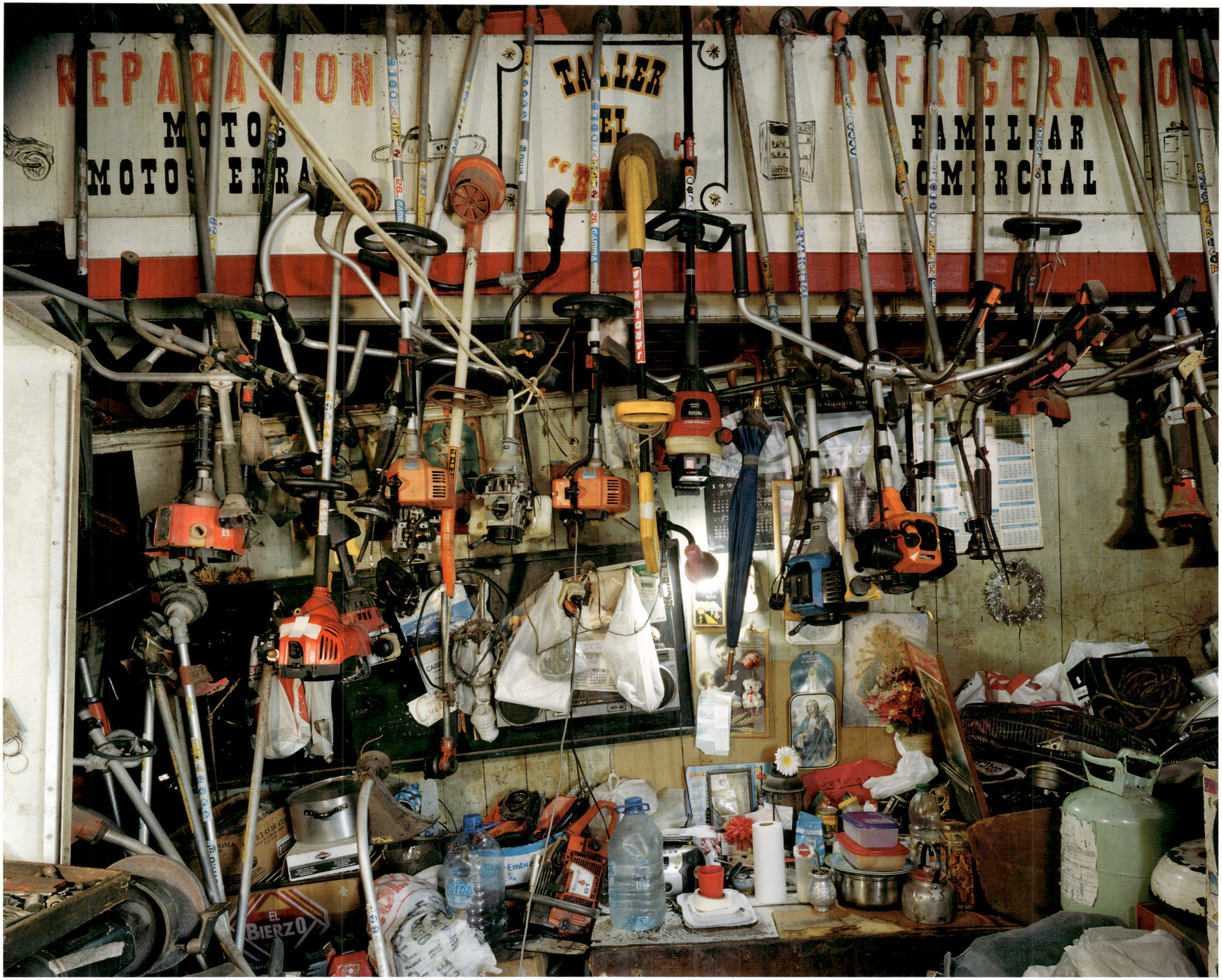
REPARACION
MOTOS
TALLER
REFRIGERACION
FAMILIAR
EL BIERZO

Grierson Refrigeration 2013 94

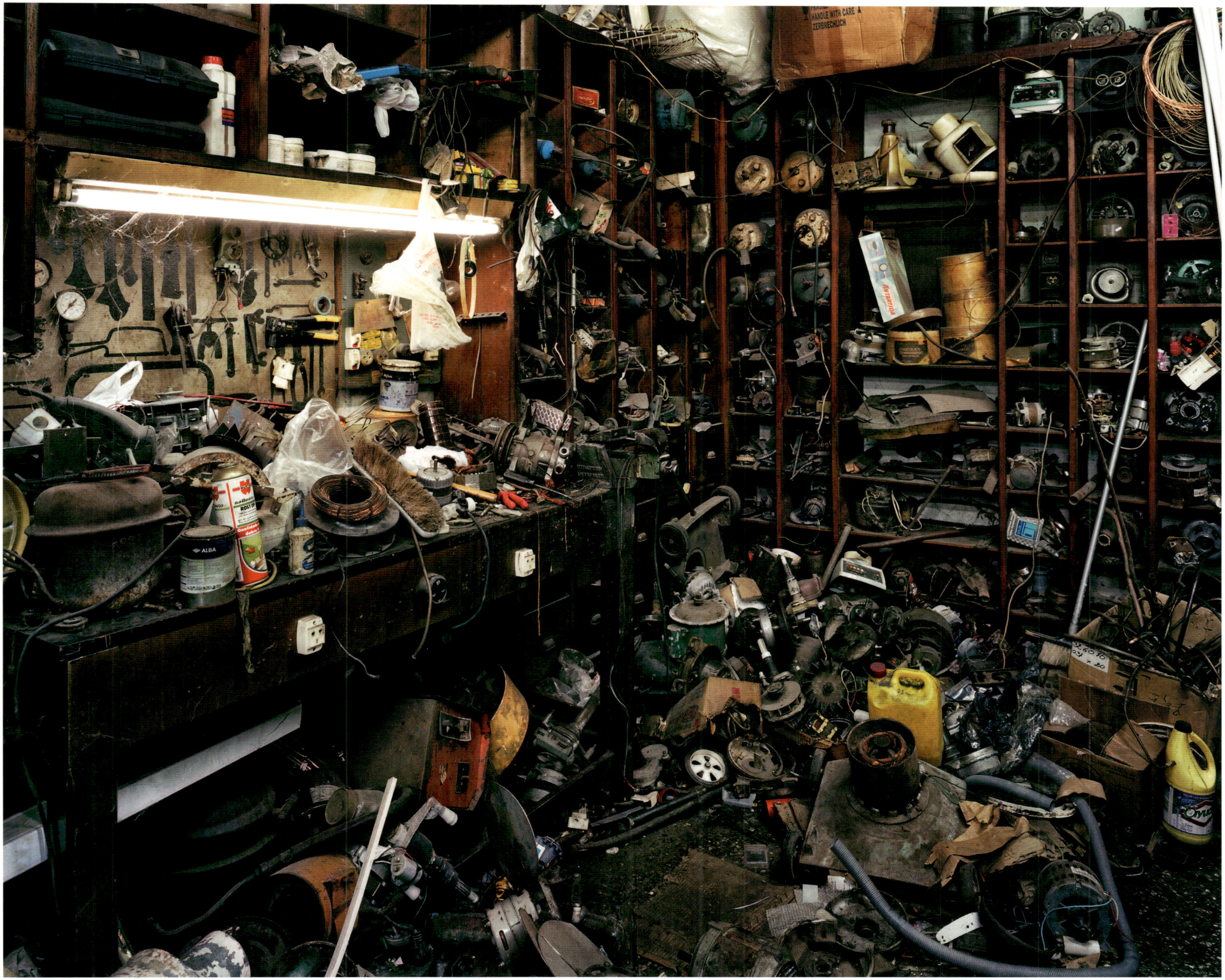
HANDLE WITH CARE
ZERBRECHLICH
ALBA

Fulgenci Shoe Repair 2013

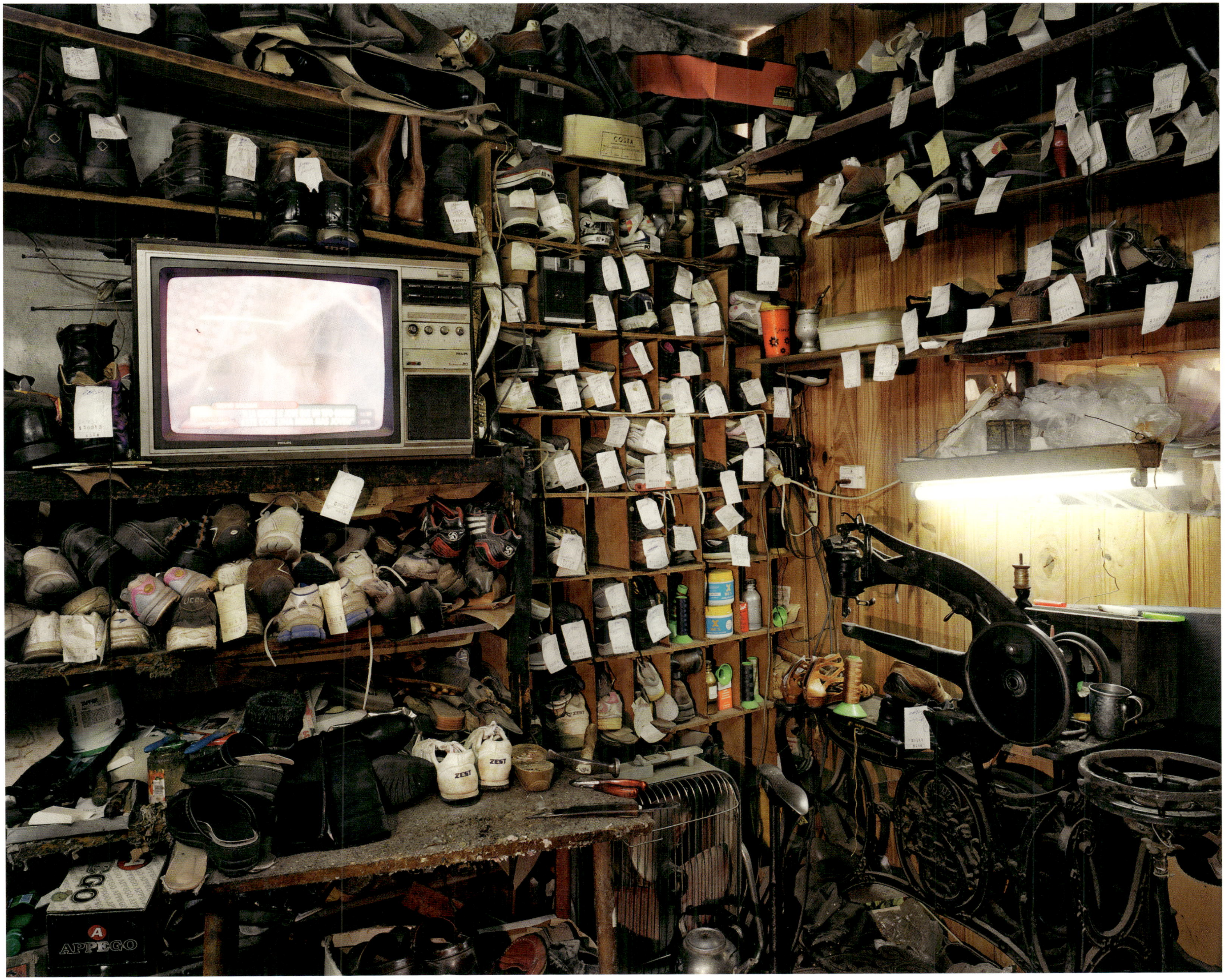
COSTA
LICEO
ZEST
ZEST
APPEGO

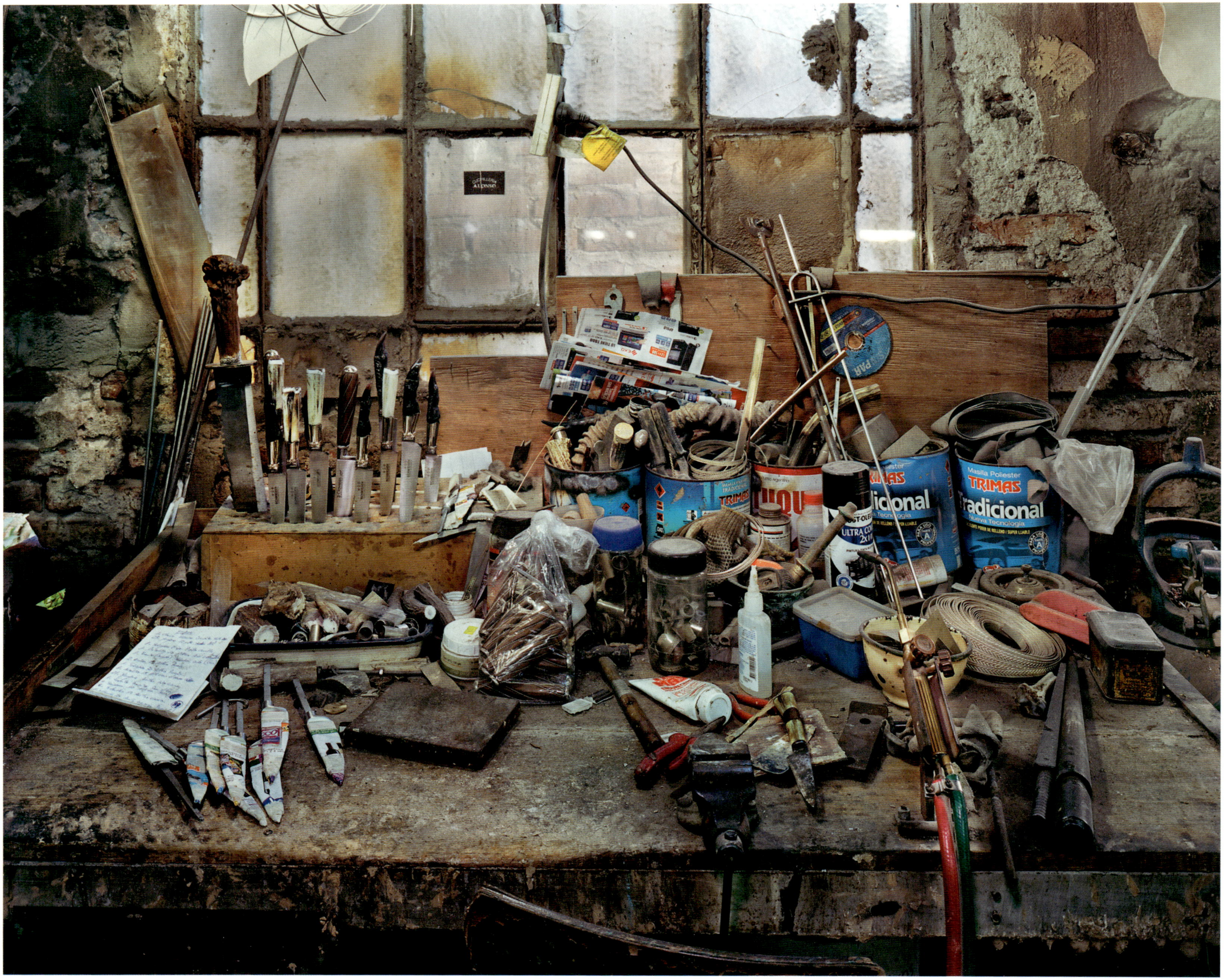
Masilla Poliester
TRIMAS
Tradicional
Nueva Tecnologia

99 **Ceferino's Workbench** 2014

Yunque Knife Factory 2014

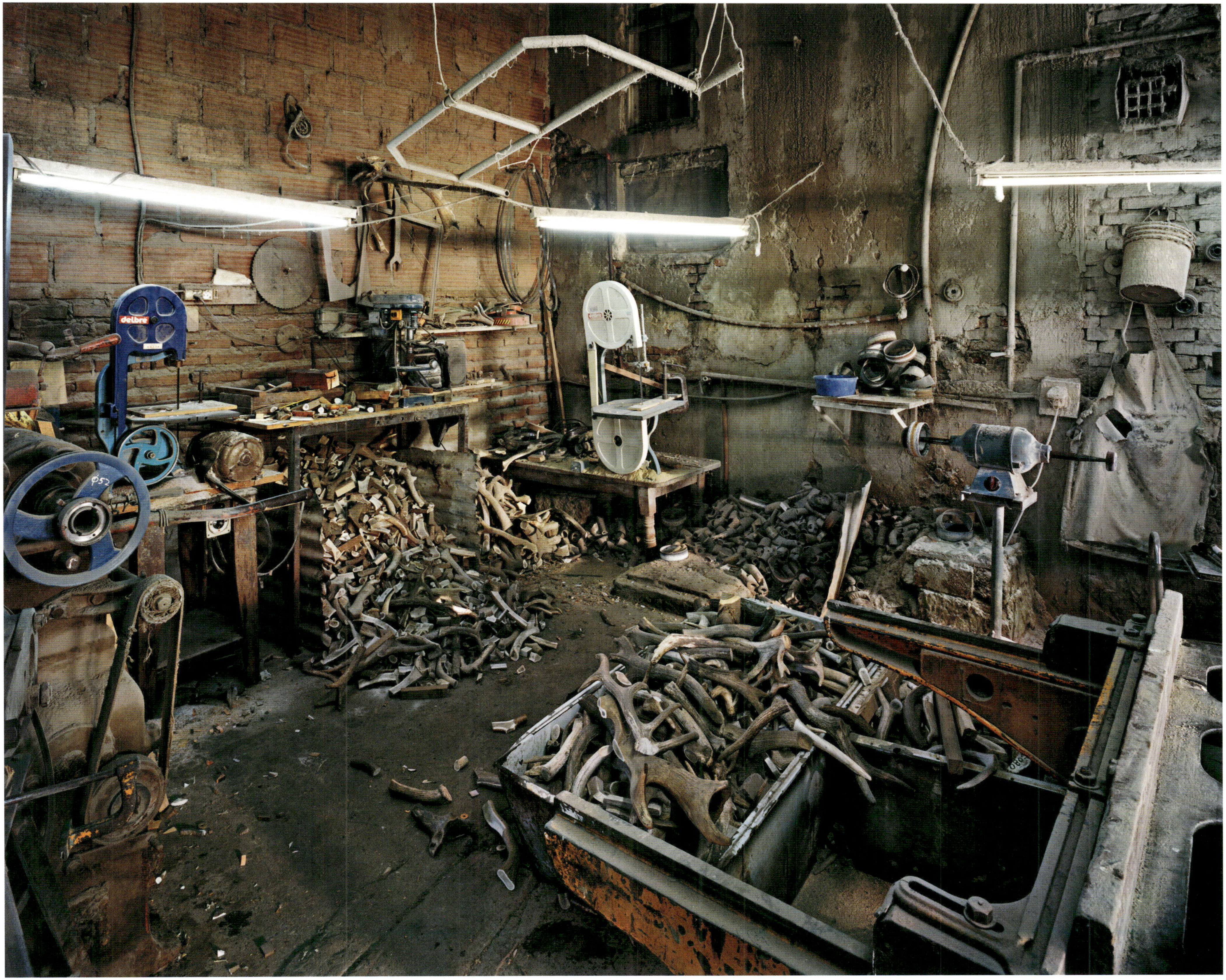
delbre

Ismaelito's Welding Shop 2013

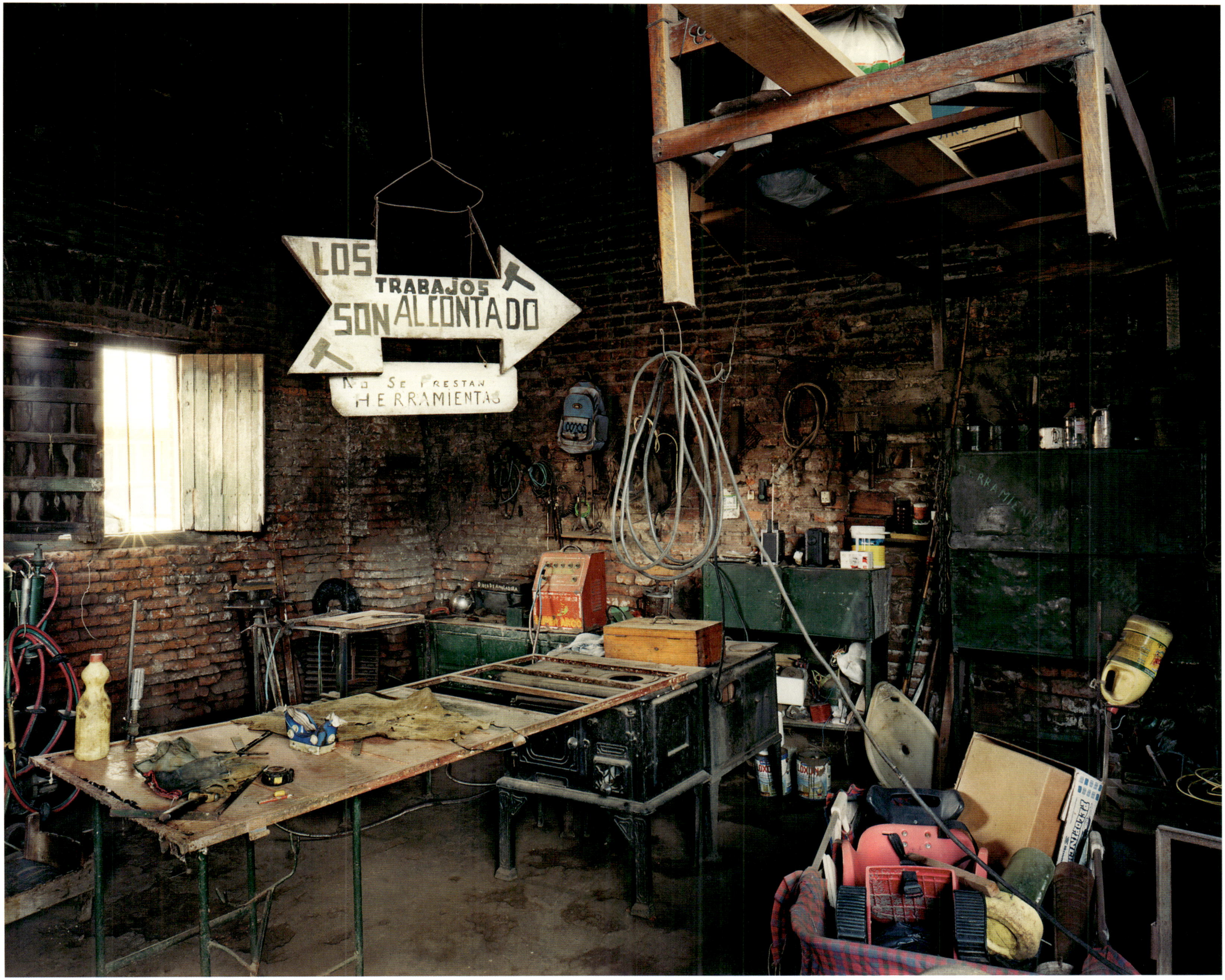
LOS TRABAJOS SON AL CONTADO
No Se Prestan HERRAMIENTAS

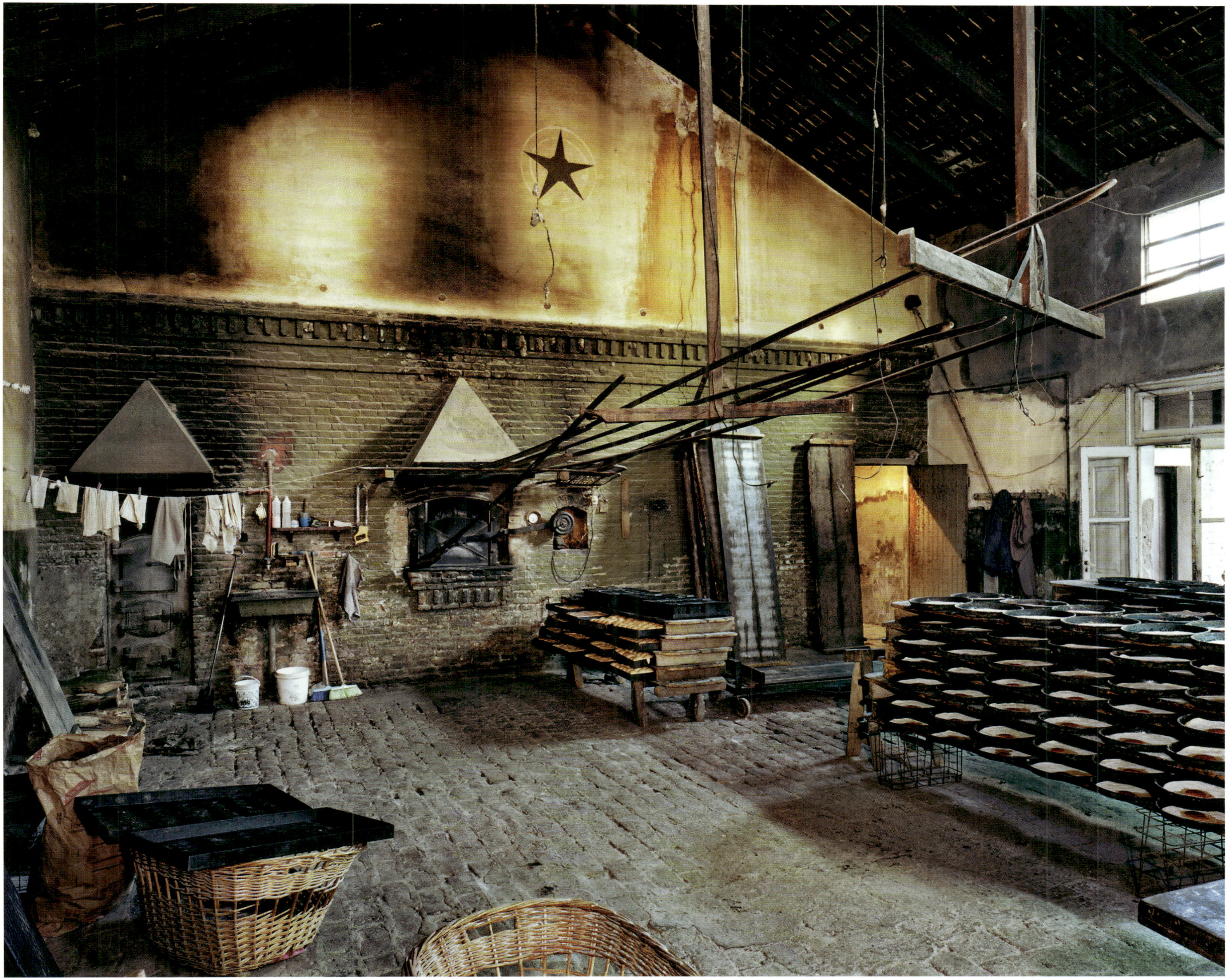

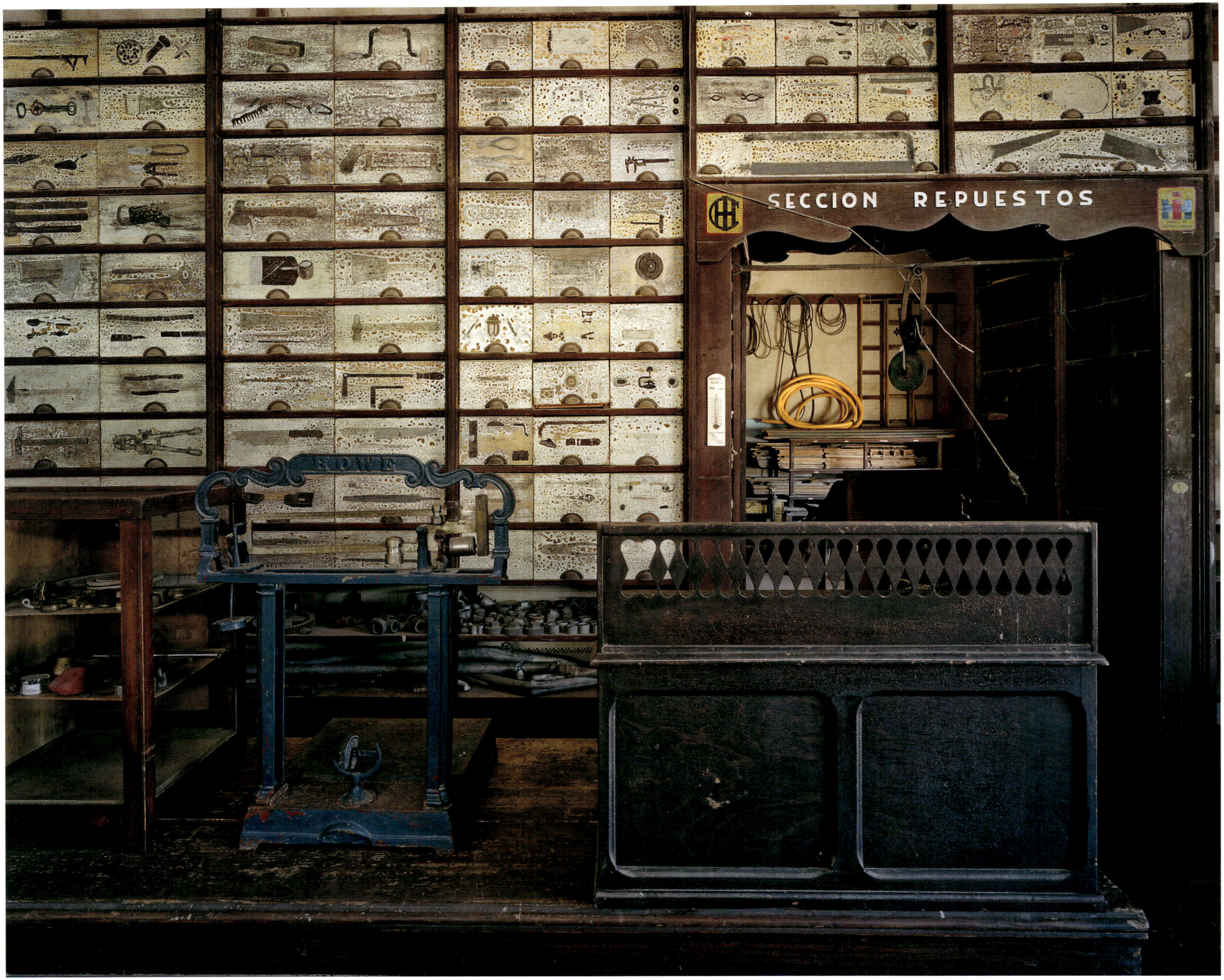
SECCION REPUESTOS
HOWE

107 **Marcelino López General Store** 2009

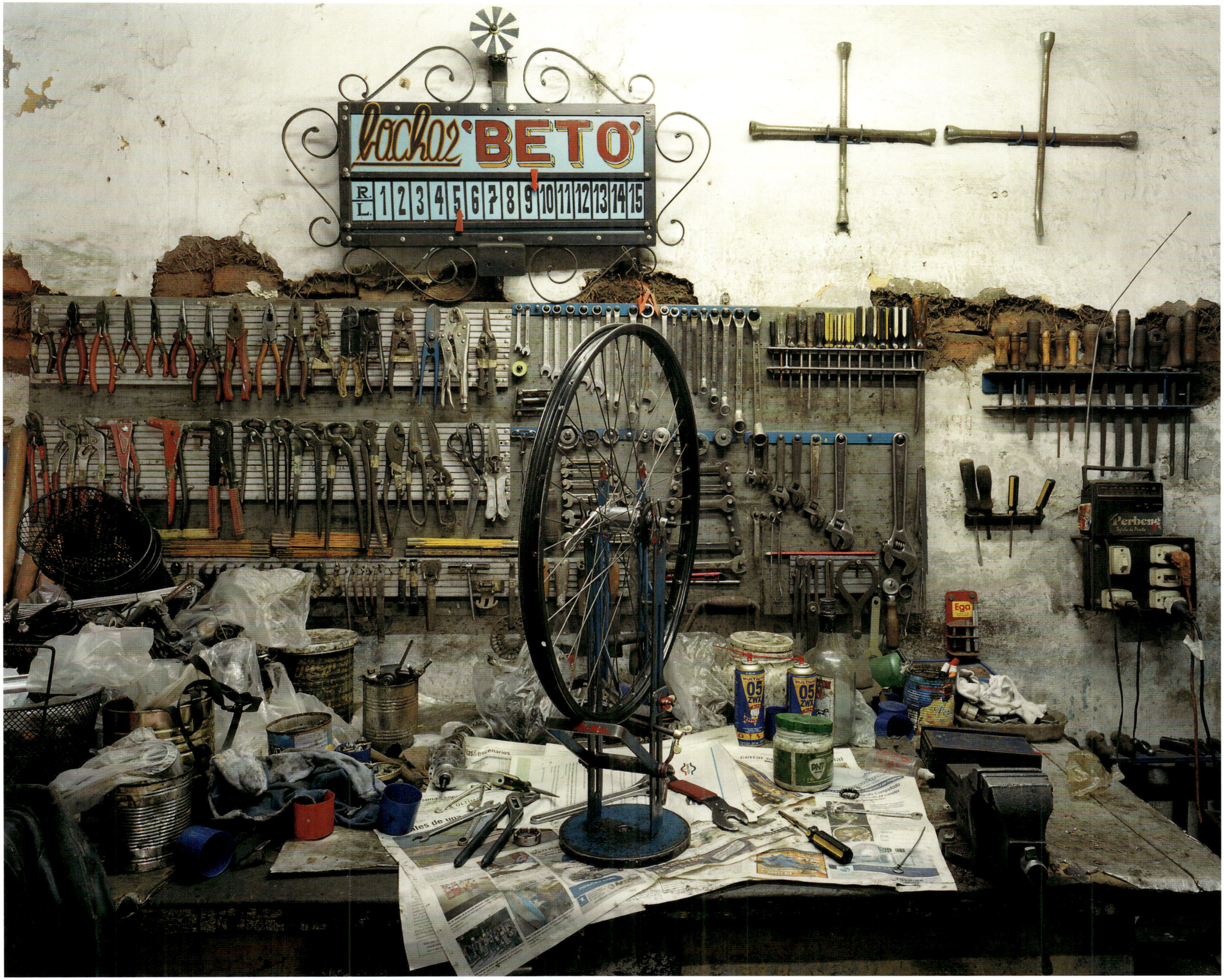

'BETO'
R L 1 2 3 4 5 6 7 8 9 10 11 12 13 14 15
Perbene
Ega

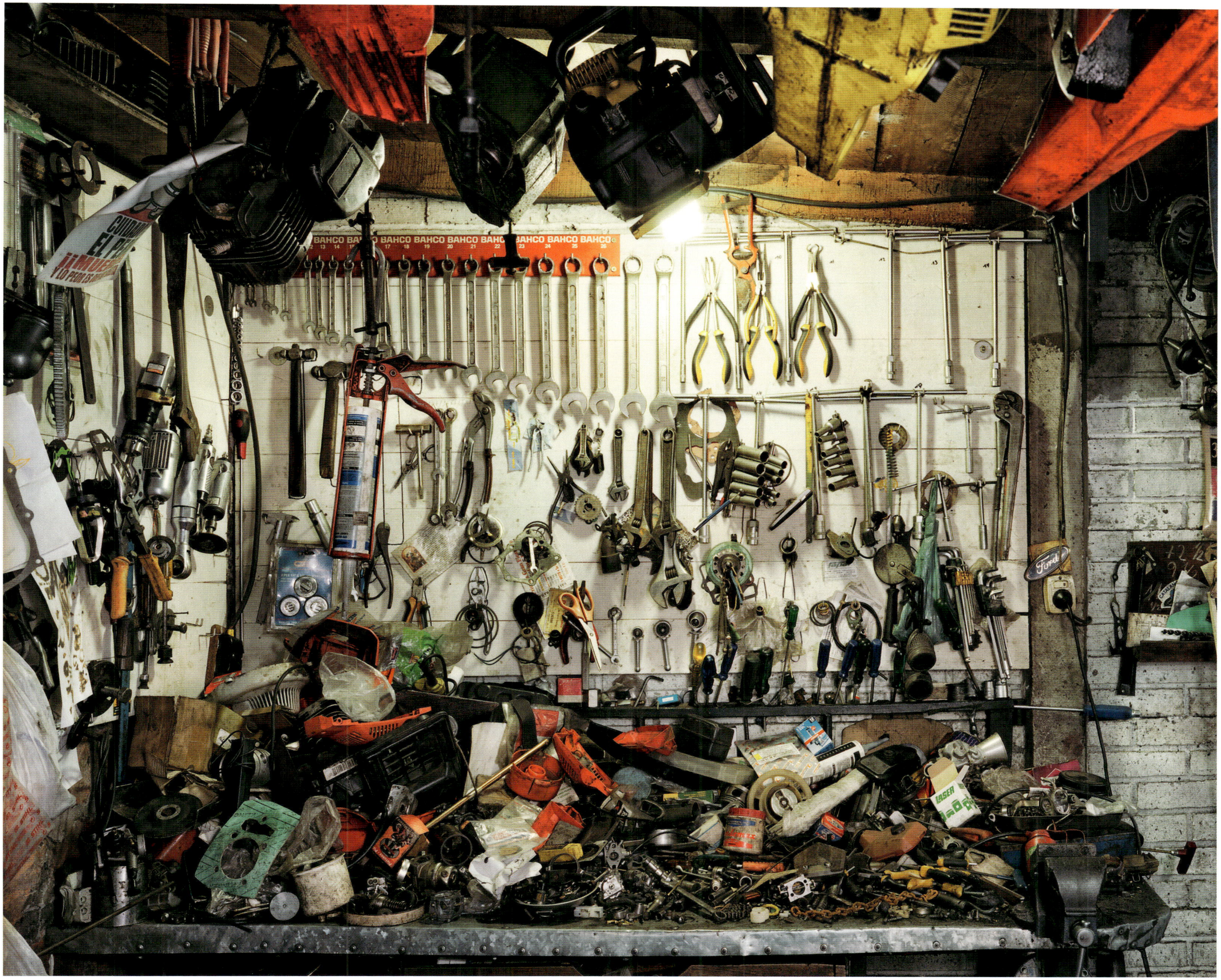
BAHCO
Ford
LASER

Raúl's Tire Repair Shop 2010

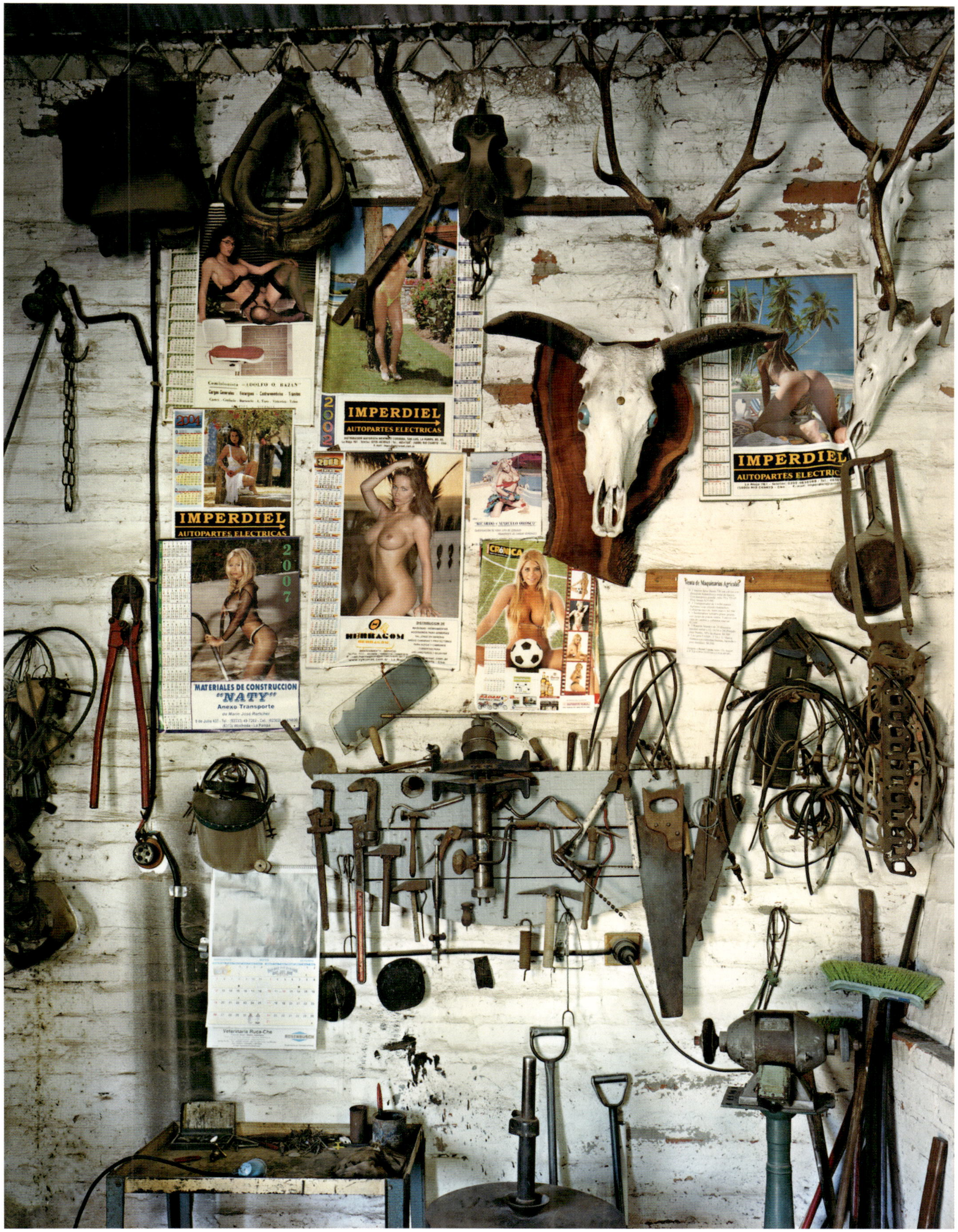
IMPERDIEL
AUTOPARTES ELECTRICAS
IMPERDIEL
AUTOPARTES ELECTRICAS
IMPERDIEL
2007
MATERIALES DE CONSTRUCCION
"NATY"
Anexo Transporte
CRÓNICA
Veterinaria Ruca-Che

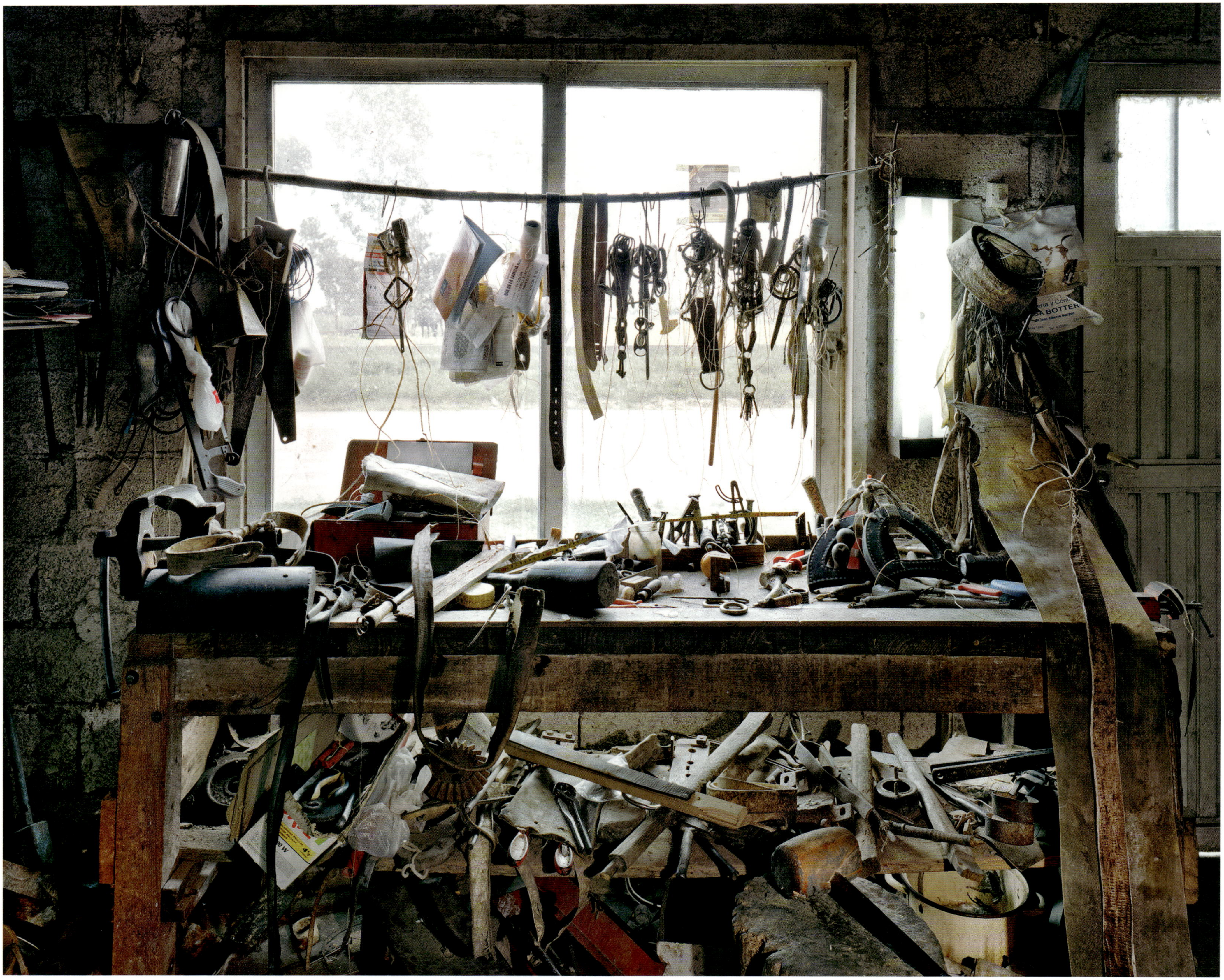

115 **Beto Cejas Rope Maker** 2013

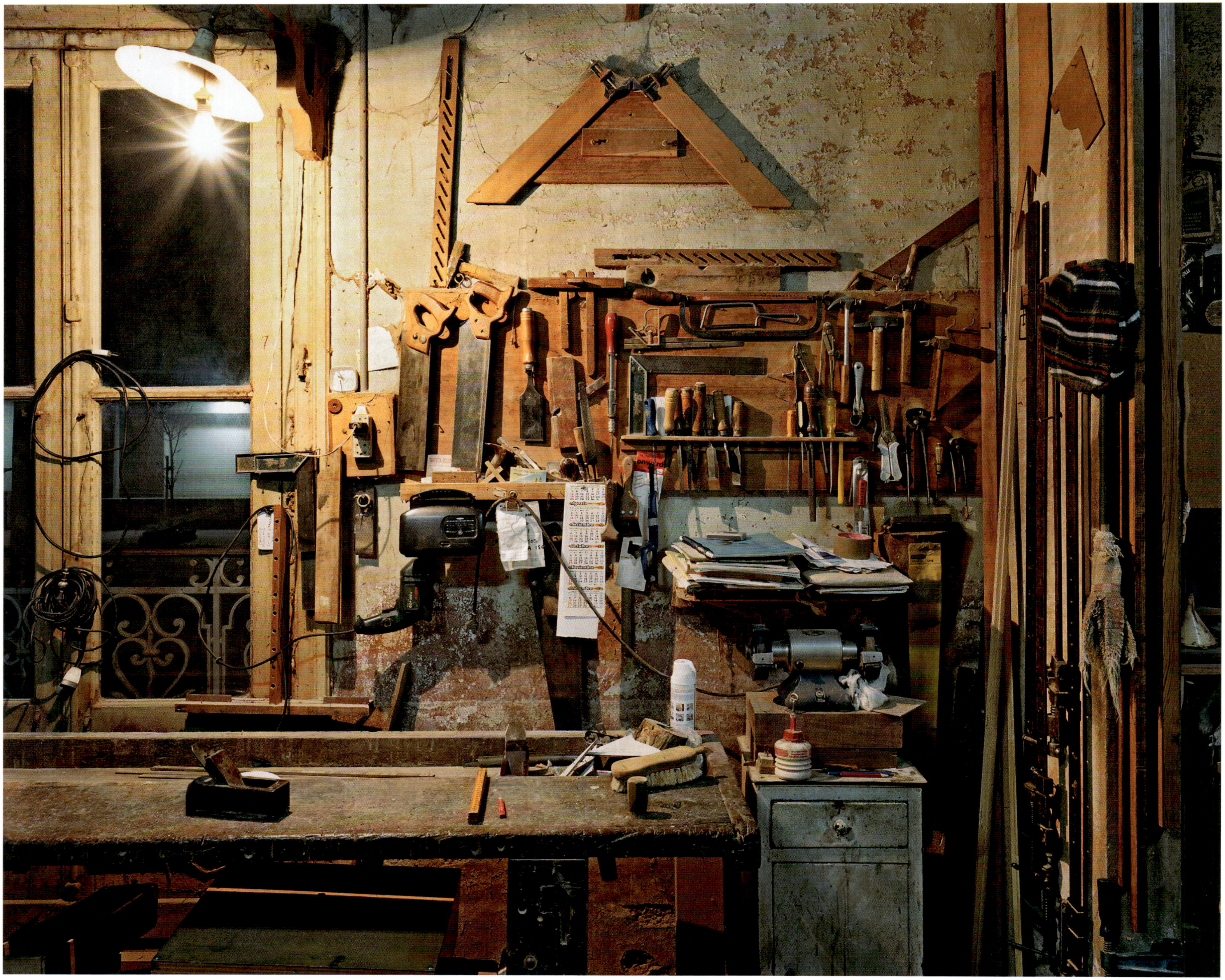

117 **Colonna Wood Shop** 2009

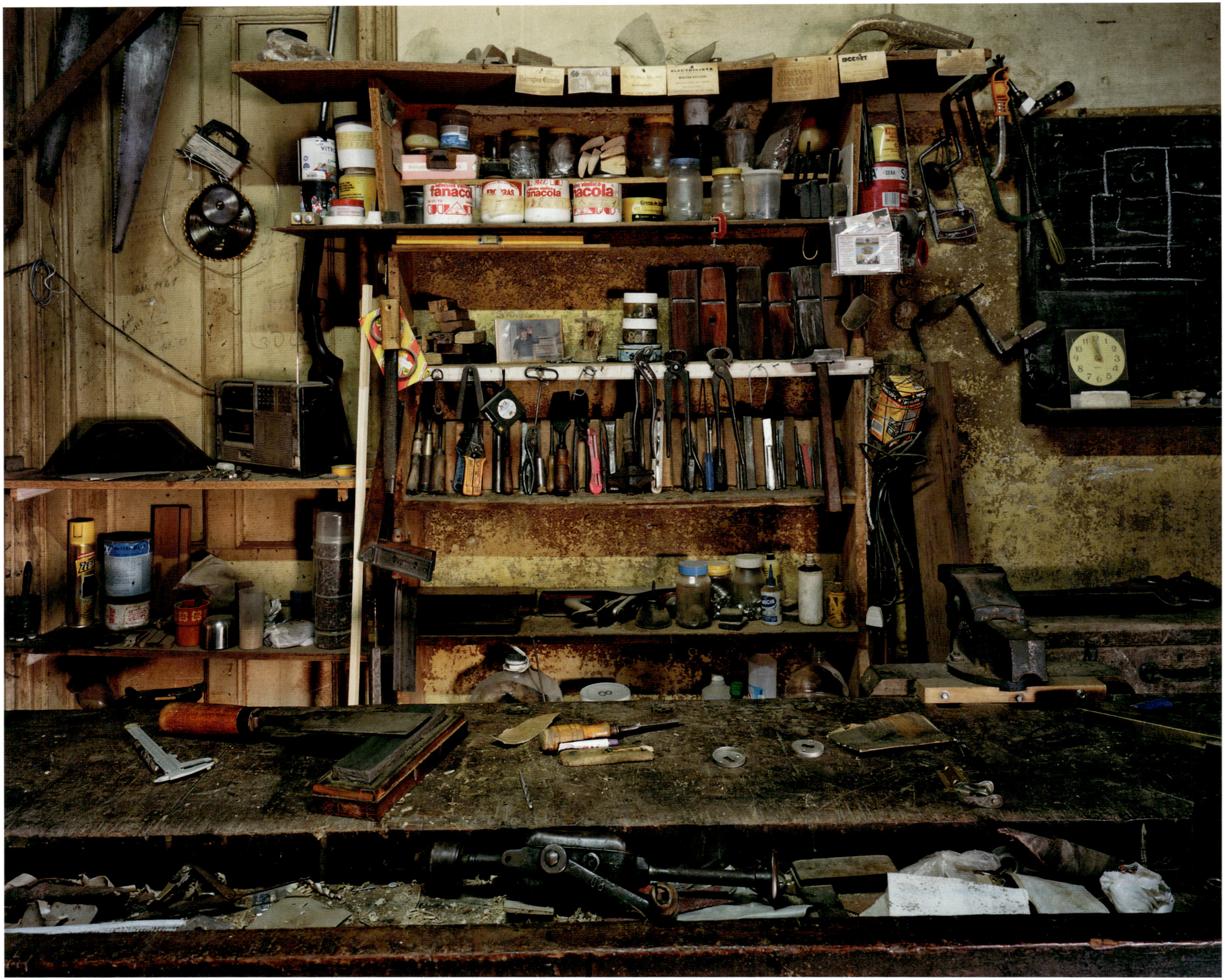
fanacol
fanacola
nacola
ELECTRICISTA
CERA

119 **Rivero's Carpentry Shop** 2013

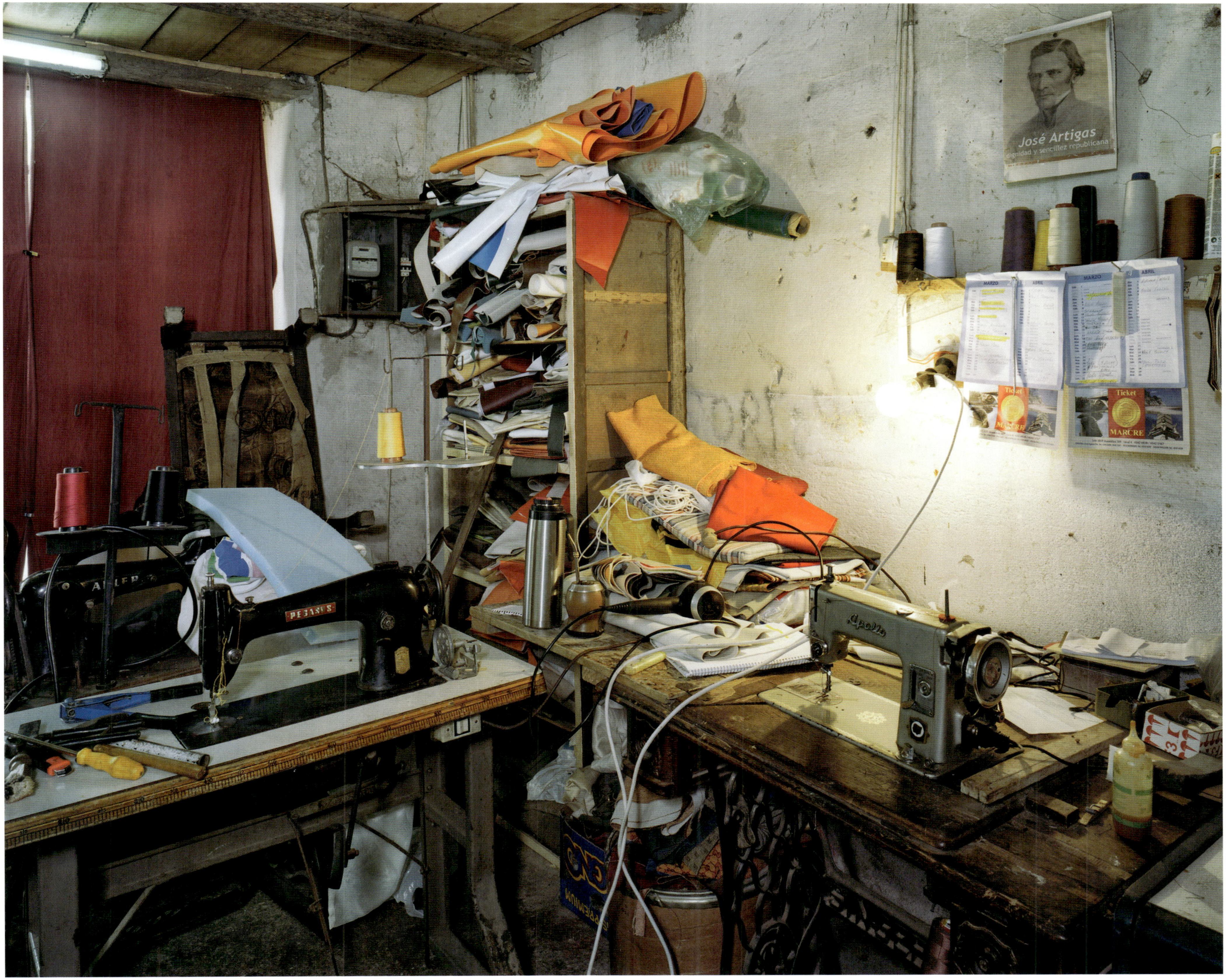
José Artigas
Ticket
MARCRE

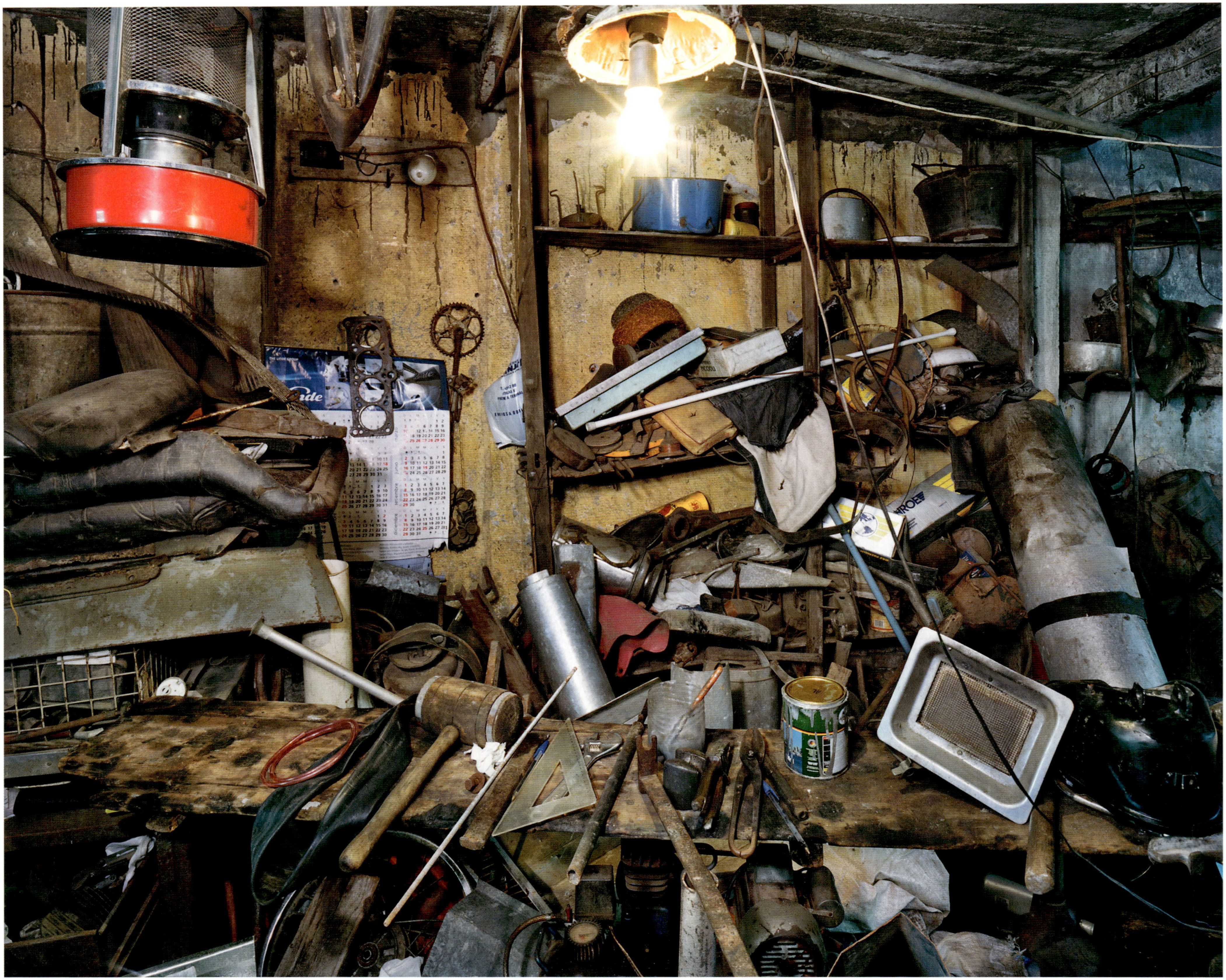

123 **El Triunfo Tinsmith Shop** 2014

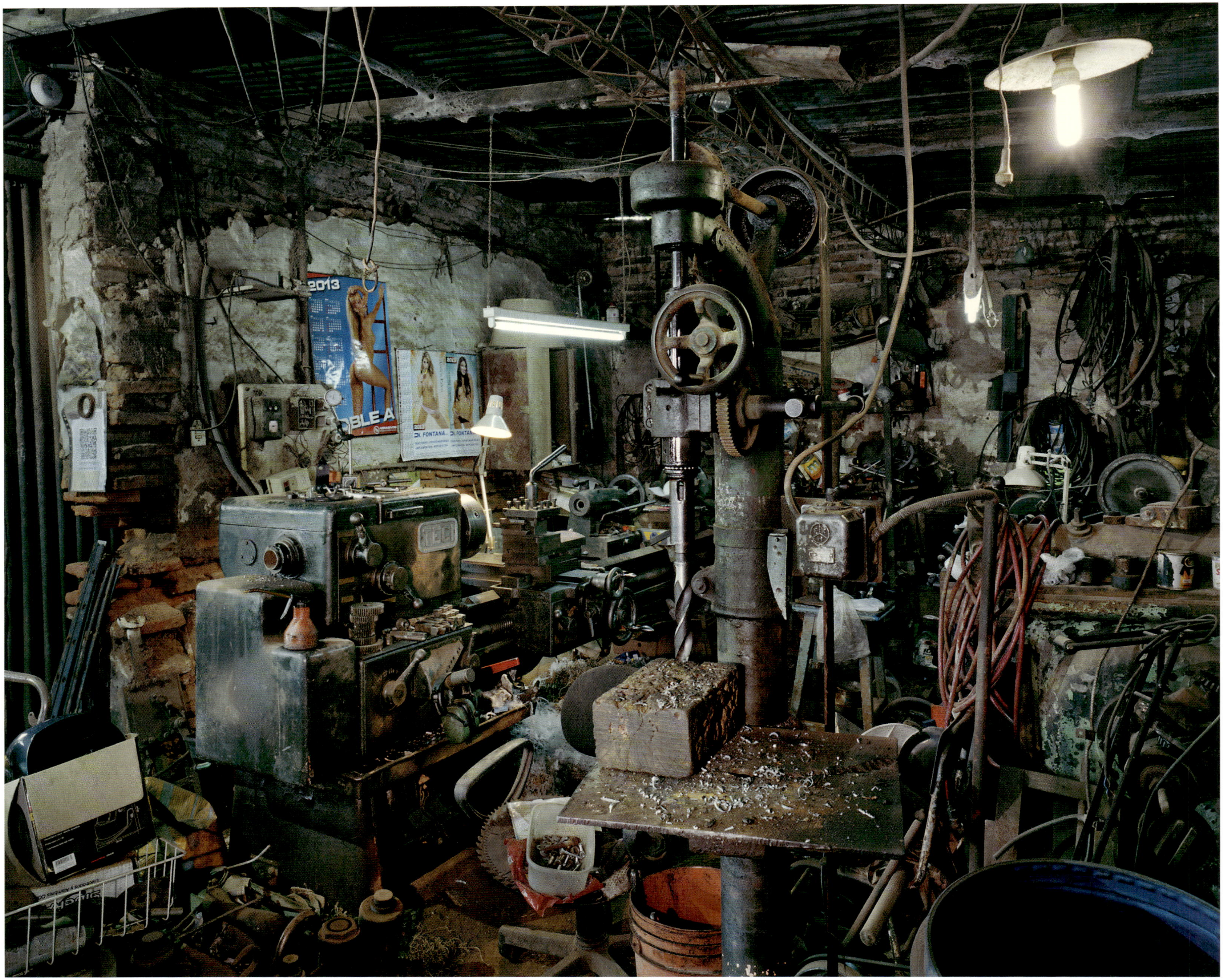
2013

125 **La Cueva** 2013

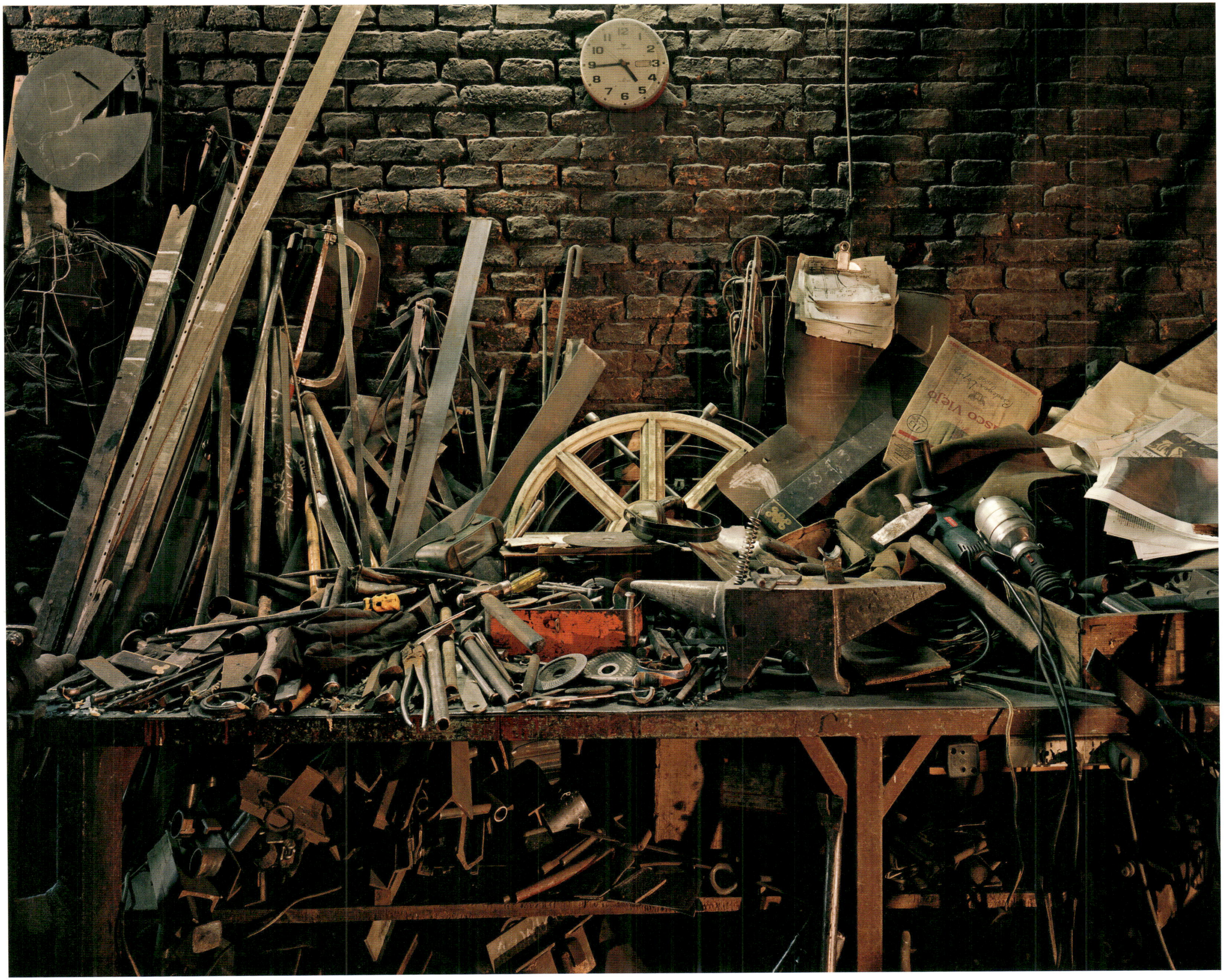

García's Broom Making Shop 2013

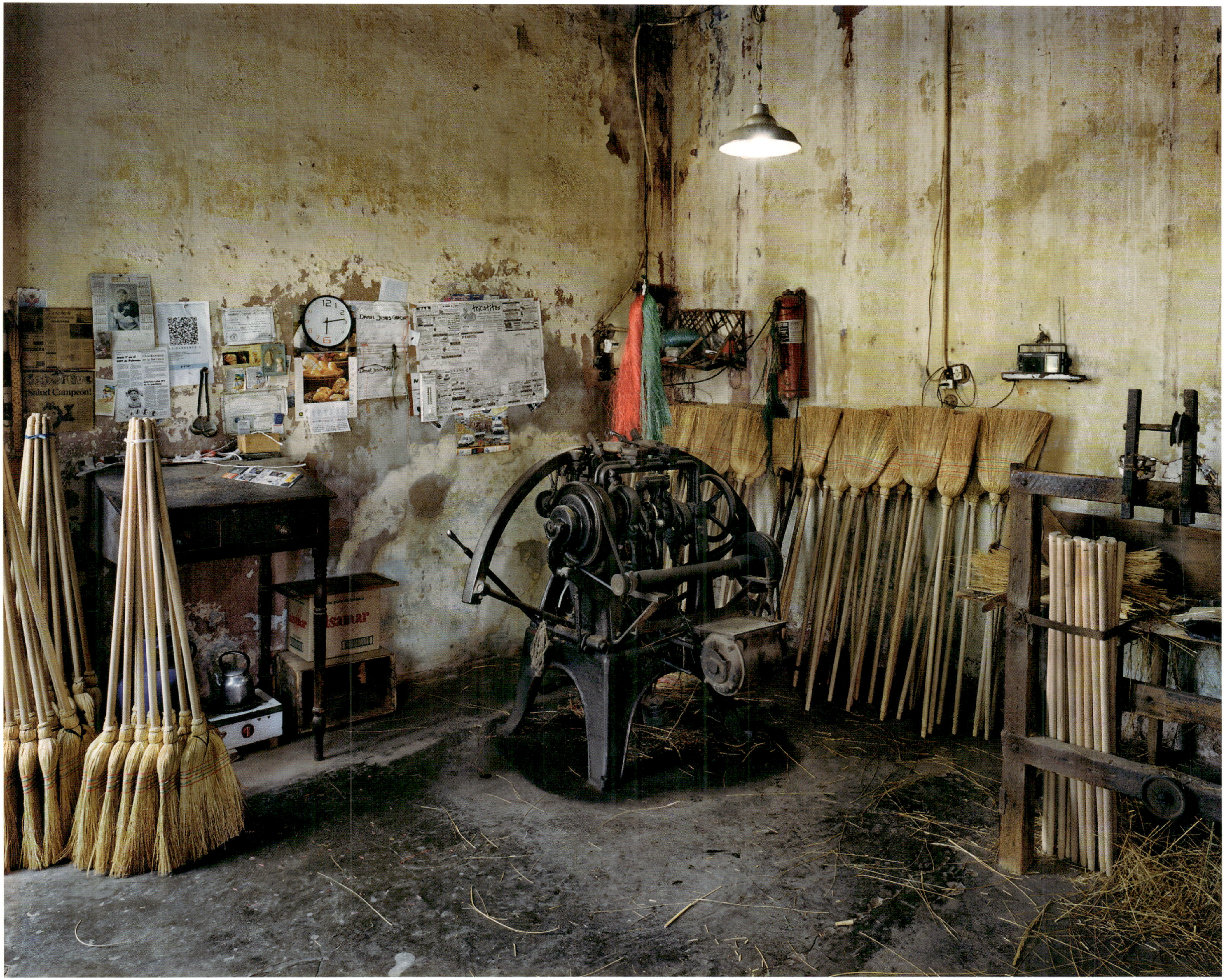

¡Salud Campeón!
tricotitos

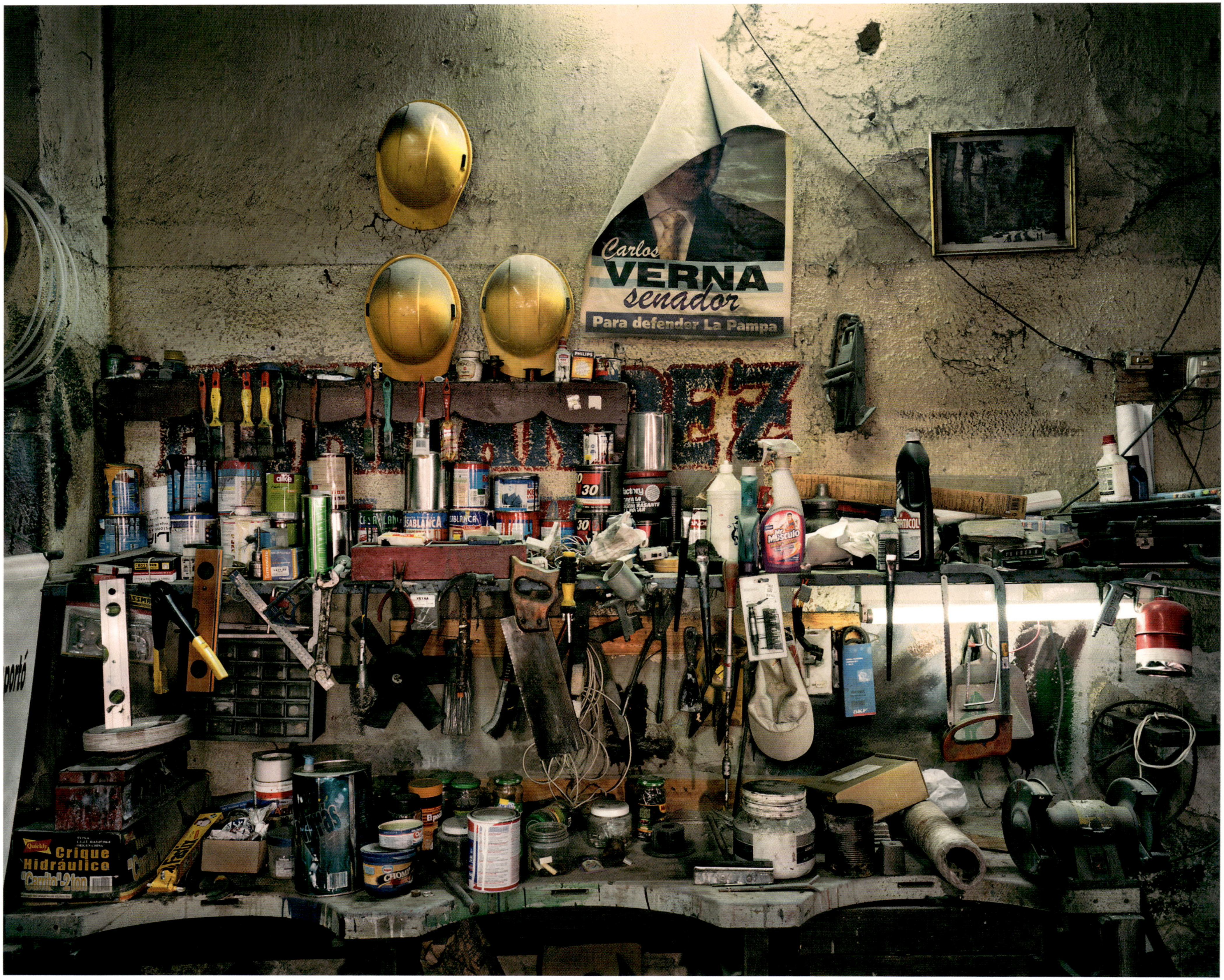
Carlos
VERNA
senador
Para defender La Pampa
Crique
Hidráulico

131 **Tucho's Sign Painting Shop** 2010

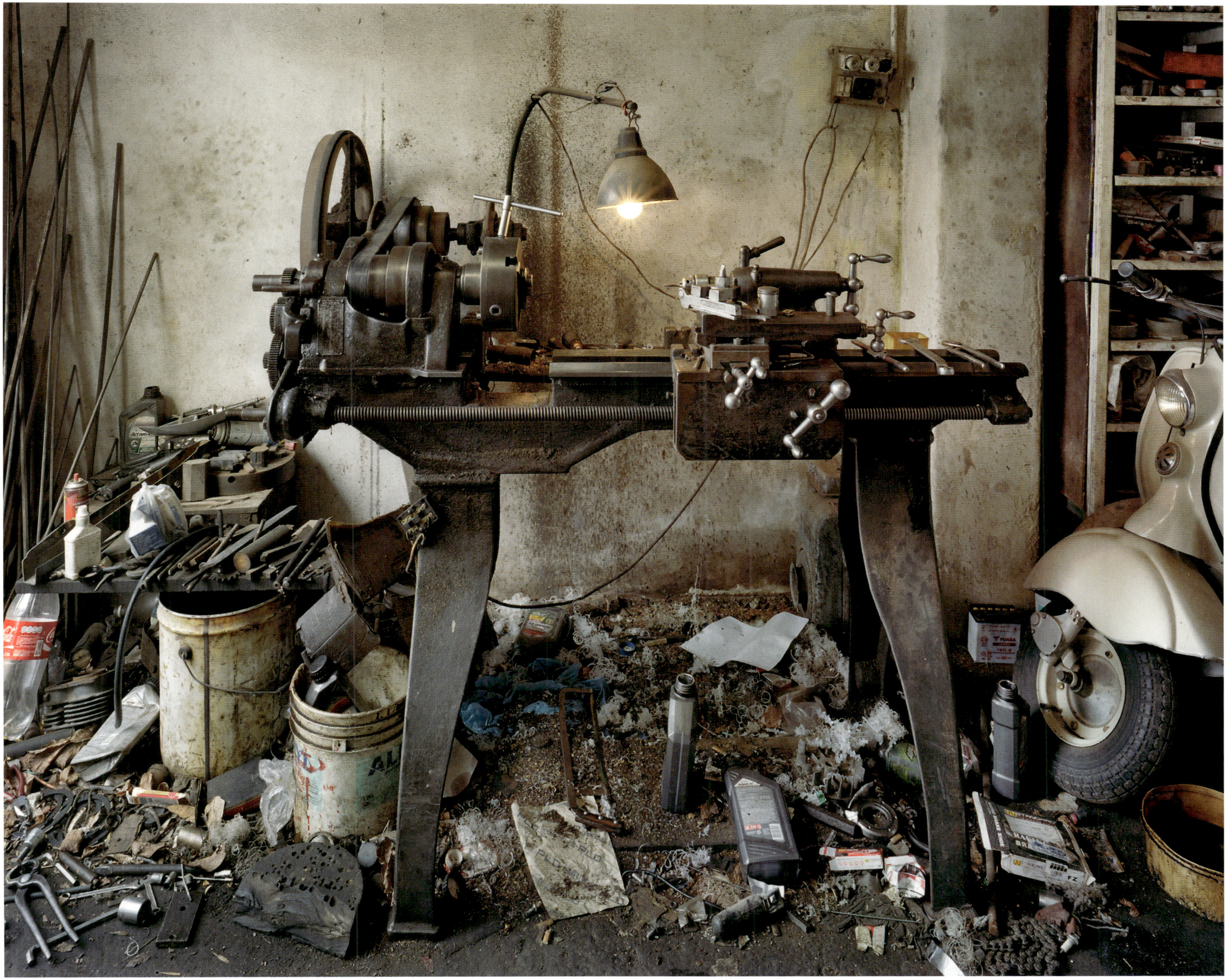

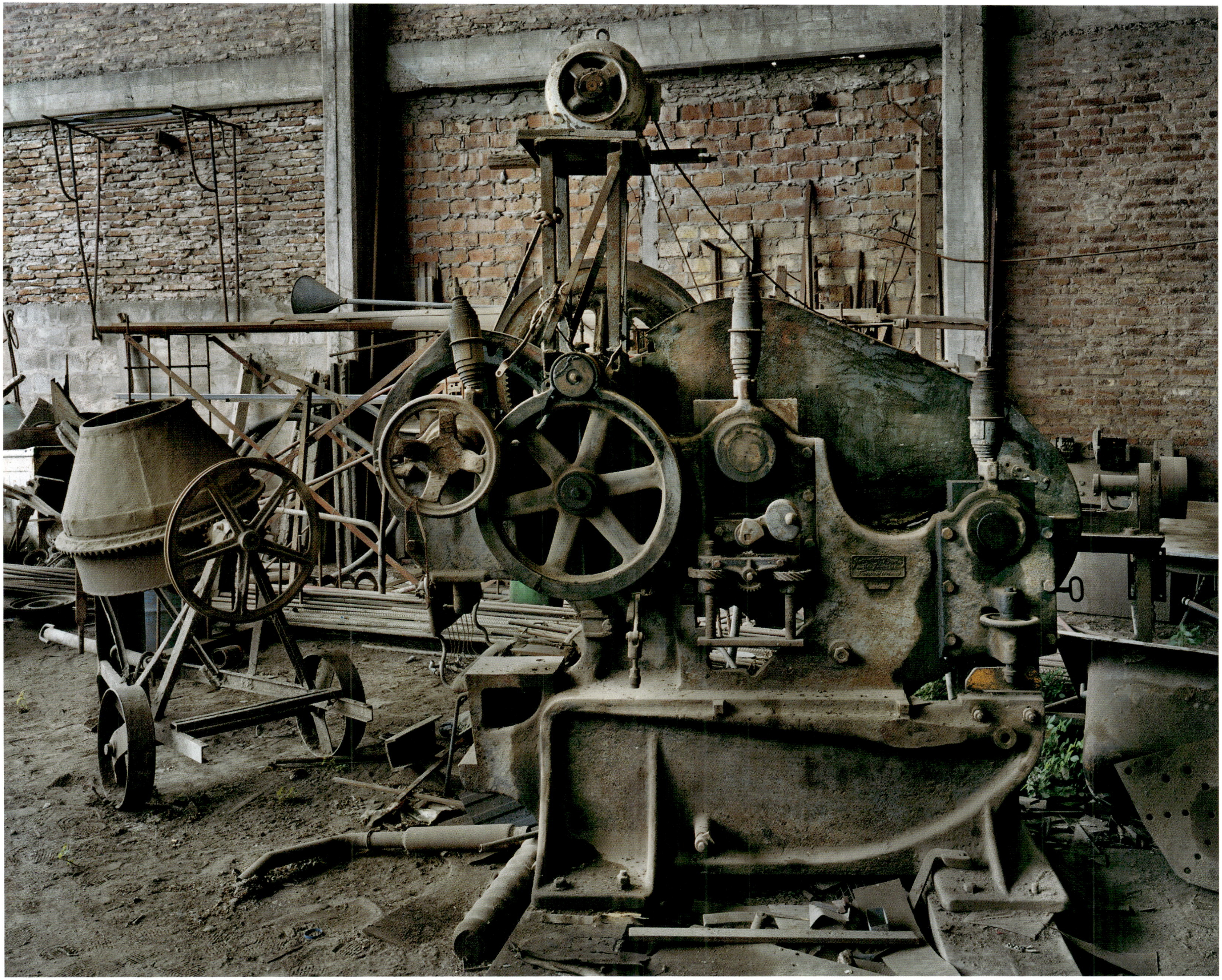

Los Pagos–The Places
Guillermo Srodek-Hart

136

I began taking these photographs in 2004 driven by an interest in the old ways of life of rural Argentina. It was evident to me that the passage of time was erasing these sites of beauty and mystery, and with them, their owners' histories. A generation of men and women whose identity is viscerally connected to what they do is slowly vanishing with their shops and businesses. Those places that still survive stand as living monuments of a disappearing way of life. They are doomed landmarks of the past. They are the last ones standing.

My grandfather's death had a lot to do with my obsession with mortality and what is left behind after someone is gone. The memories I treasure the most are the stories he would tell me of his own personal history. The objects of his that I have kept—clothes and photographs, watches, hearing aids—all have a value because of the person he once was. Together with my memories, it is all that remains.

Alberto Lindt owns the Leili bike shop in the town of Moisesville, but he is also the sole engraver of tombstones in Yiddish in the entire province of Santa Fe. The day I took the picture, I randomly pointed at one of the tombstones and asked him if he would translate the text for me. He said it was a traditional saying within the Jewish community: "The life of the dead is placed in the memory of the living."

In these ten years of photographing, I have witnessed radical changes in many of the places that I have visited and documented. Some have closed and been subsequently demolished. An example is Bar Firpo in Tandil, a four-and-a-half-hour drive south of Buenos Aires. The day I photographed it, the guy running the bar told me that there had recently been a legal settlement by which the owner had decided to sell the bar, split the money among the heirs, and move on. This was a place where old guys had gathered for years, maybe lifetimes, to play cards, watch soccer, have a drink, and socialize.

The afternoon I took the picture, one fellow walked in and sat in his usual spot to read the paper, the way he always did at that same time of the day. Because he was going deaf he couldn't hear the others telling him to move out of the frame. It was such a ritualized behavior that he was oblivious to the fact that a large camera was being pointed straight at him. Bar Firpo, like many others, serves as a second home for these guys who embed themselves into the space; they define it, they own it.

Months later I went back to give the bartender a copy of the picture and to find out what was going on with the closure. The front was shuttered but I could hear people laughing and chatting inside. I slapped the metal blinds and the bartender came out from the side of the building. He was happy to see me and was pleased with the print. I asked him what was going on with the bar and he said, "Your timing is perfect. We were just having our farewell toast.

Tomorrow the contract expires and we will be closing for good. I don't know what will happen to the bar. All I know is that we have to leave." I recently found out that the Bar Firpo had been bought by a well-known family from the area and was turned into a restaurant. I drove by to see it with my own eyes. The building was still there but the interior was different. The place was filled with tables and the walls were overdecorated. It had been cleaned up. I asked what had happened to the regulars that used to hang out at the bar, and the new owner said that they were never to be seen again.

Social change can also act as a destructive force. Juan Carlos was the owner of "El 91" butcher shop in Las Flores. He told me how, when he first started, he would deliver the freshly cut meat, wrapped in newspaper, door to door, in a cart pulled by horses. Later he managed to buy the corner from his employers and became the head butcher. For the rest of his life he sold the meat straight from the marble counter. By the time he was in his eighties new sanitary regulations made it mandatory for butcher shops to use temperature-controlled refrigerators. Juan Carlos was selling meat the old way and had done so all his life. It was too late to change. He had never had a customer complain about his meat not being fresh, nor had anyone gotten sick from eating it. Having no one interested in carrying on with the trade and too old to make the investment, Juan Carlos was forced to close the "El 91" butcher shop. He went home and soon became ill. The last time I knocked on his door, his wife told me he had recently died. We hugged on the sidewalk as she cried.

As time goes by, these places become harder and harder to find. I might start following an itinerary based on past locations that remained pending from another trip, or sometimes I will go somewhere just out of curiosity, perhaps because I heard something about that town on the radio or read about it in a book. During the long drives, I find shrines on the side of the highways devoted mostly to the Gauchito Gil and the Difunta Correa, the two most popular pagan saints in Argentina. Contrary to the places I am photographing, the shrines seem to be growing and multiplying. I find them fascinating in their collaborative and dynamic nature. No shrine will look the same from one week to the next. They are in constant flux, the result of anonymous people leaving their offerings, anything from a written letter to a vehicle, symbolizing a fulfilled promise or a future wish to be granted. The shrines to these two popular saints keep me company as I drive to the next town. Once I arrive, I look for the old façades, hoping I might find something inside, or catch a glimpse through a window, or feel the need to get out of the truck and spy through an old wooden blind. I might randomly walk into a place with my portfolio under my arm, which often makes people think I am a tax collector. I will then introduce myself as a photographer looking for old stores still functioning "as it used to be," open my folio of pictures, and ask for their help in finding them. They get it right away; they understand the kinds of places I am looking for and point me in some direction, and that is how I find them.

But it doesn't always work out well. One time, when I was in Uriburu, La Pampa, in Bar El Mate, I was looking at my pictures with a bunch of regulars who were having a late afternoon drink. Among them was Tucho, a sign painter who convinced me to drive three hours across the desert to a town called Chacharramendi, in the direction of Patagonia. He was absolutely sure I was going to find the most unbelievable old general store I could possibly imagine. Apparently the place was still functioning from the times of the Indian wars. I asked him if it was the real deal and not a museum, and he said, "Trust me, you will not regret it." He even said that if I had any problems I could mention his name to the town mayor. "Tell him Tucho sent you, he knows me well." Tucho was so convincing that the next morning I decided to go to Chacharramendi. I drove three hours southwest across the desert in the heat of a summer day. When I finally made it, I ran to take a look through the window. My heart sunk. The place had historic objects from the past labeled with computer printouts and arranged in the most perfunctory fashion. It was a tourist trap. I went in just to make sure I was seeing right, and left without taking a picture. Instead, I drove the long distance back to my hotel cursing Tucho (and myself) all the while.

As I try to find and photograph these places, I have been a witness to their demise. I feel I am losing the race. Why is this happening? A big part of it is due to the fact that they stand alone. No one takes care of them except their owners. Their passion and love and their connection to their place is the engine that keeps them going. The people who run these establishments feel their entire self is defined by what they do and where they are. It is their *lugar en el mundo*, their place in the world. Yet they are treated as obstacles in a frenetic race toward an uncertain future. This, to my eyes, makes them true rebels, standing by themselves with their beliefs and ways of living, which is why I am so endeared to them. They are who they are and they will not change; as the world around them goes in other directions, and despite time playing against them, there is no retirement. They will go on until they die, and when they do, these places will most likely die with them.

Guillermo Srodek-Hart with Silvestre, owner of
La Mariana General Store, and a regular.

Mapis, Buenos Aires Province, 2014

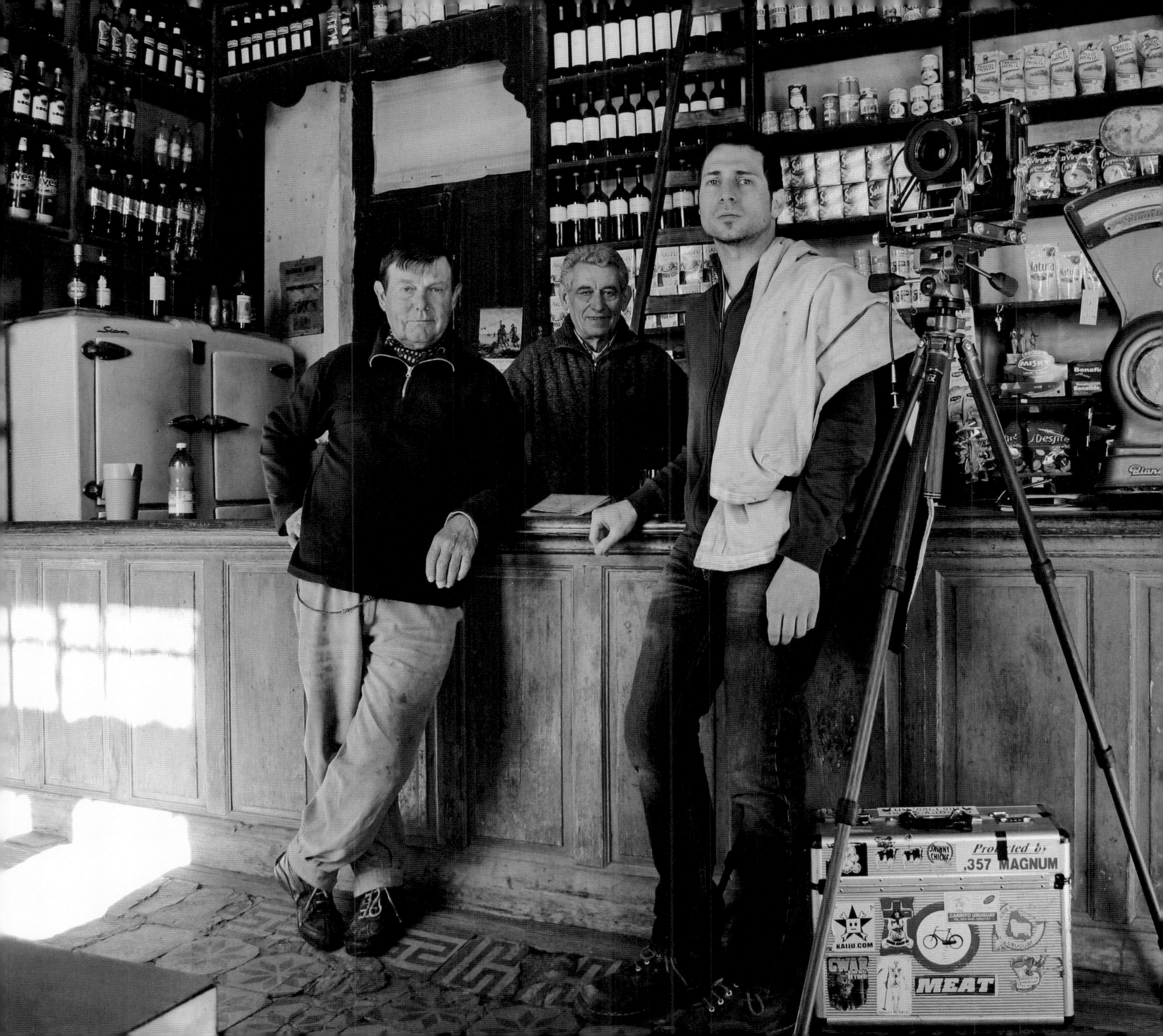
Protected by
.357 MAGNUM
MEAT

Extended Captions

El Zorro 2005

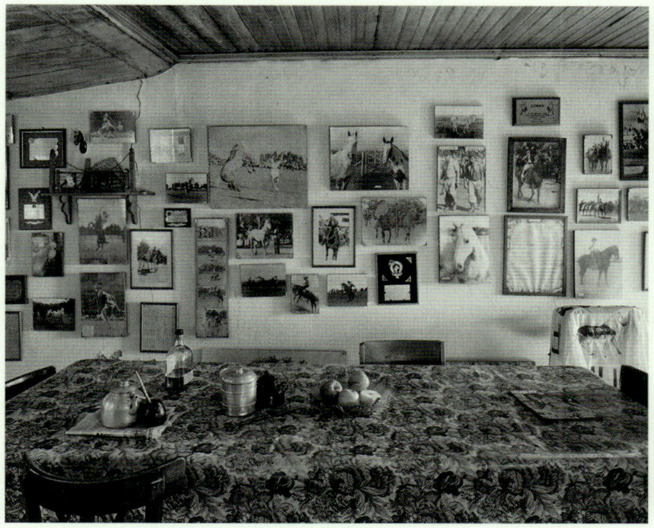

El Zorro was the best rodeo horse in Argentine history. His fame grew as he competed in the so-called *jineteadas*, mostly in the province of Buenos Aires. He would toss riders like rag dolls. In one sad episode, he accidently killed one of them in front of hundreds of spectators. His fame grew even more. Zorro died when he was twenty-eight years old. The horse is a legend within gaucho circles and beyond. Omar Passarotti, the horse's owner, has commemorated Zorro's life by building him a shrine in his dining room.

Cascallares, Buenos Aires Province

page 7

Bar Tito 2013

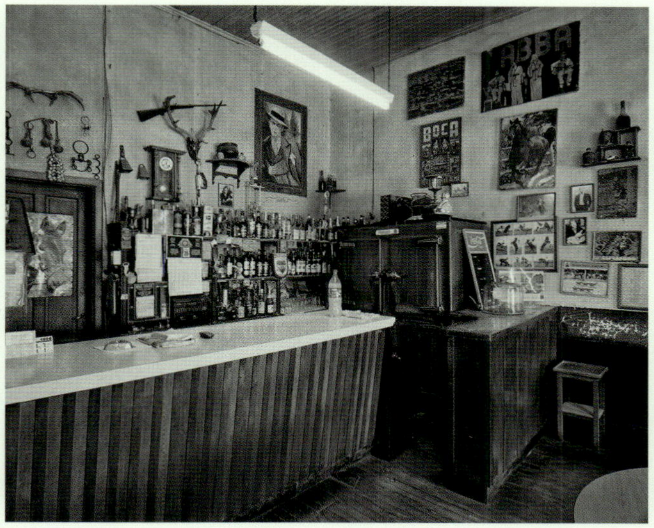

The owner of Bar Tito had had a medical problem and was unable to continue with the business. One of her sons was left in charge, but only worked on Saturdays, when the train arrives from the nearest cities full of people eager to take pictures and have a drink in an authentic farm bar. The rest of the week Gumercindo Arquímedes Rivero, a former tractor driver, is in charge of the place. As we were chatting, he looked at his watch, stood up, poured a glass of cane rum, left it on the far right of the counter, and came back to the table, leaving the tiny glass by itself. I wondered what that was all about. Minutes later, the door opened and one of the regulars walked in, sat in a chair where the glass had been left, and started sipping.

Vela, Buenos Aires Province

page 13

Bar El Mate 2010

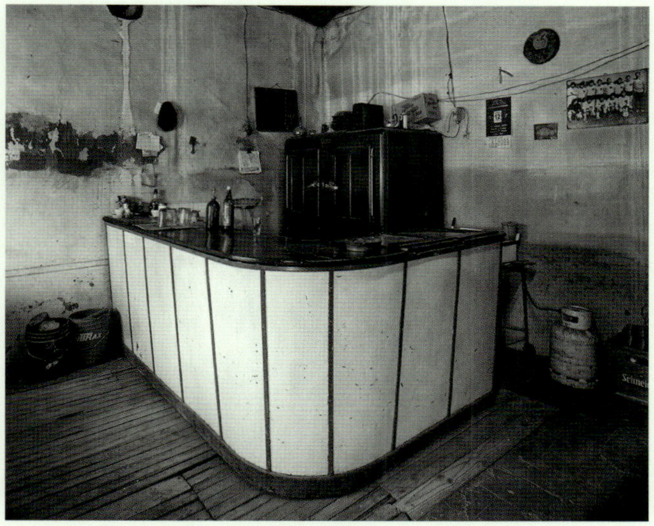

I spotted Bar El Mate from my truck. There was a table with a bunch of guys having drinks as the sun was coming down. From what I saw, the bar was worth taking a closer look, so I parked and walked up with my portfolio under my arm. At first no one was answering my questions until the owner, Raúl, asked me if I was a tax collector. I convinced him that I was only taking pictures, and he allowed me inside.

Uriburu, La Pampa Province

page 15

Bar Bessonart 2011

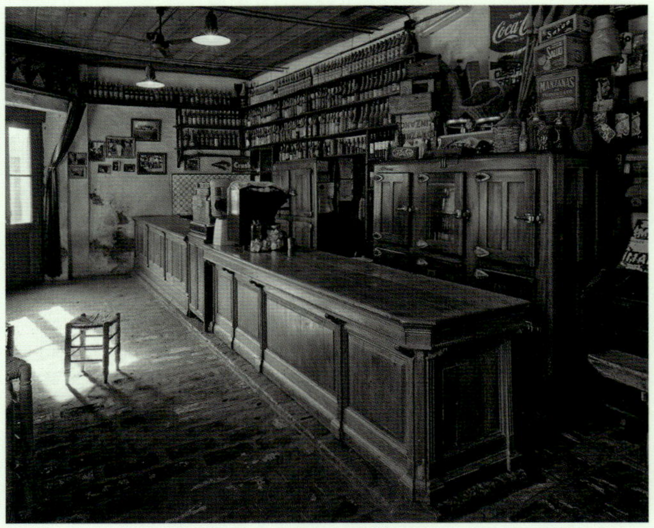

One of the most relevant literary texts written about the gauchos is called *Don Segundo Sombra*, dating from 1926. Its author, Ricardo Güiraldes, was inspired by Don Segundo Ramírez, a gaucho who used to hang out in this old bar.

San Antonio de Areco, Buenos Aires Province

page 17

Bar Melón 2014

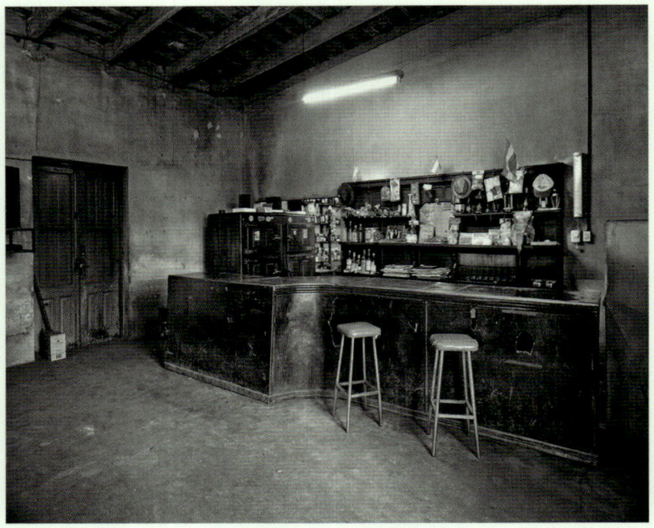

Melón got his nickname because when he was a baby his head was the size of a melon. He told me a story about how a horse got accidently shot at the bar. It happened one night when the local police officer dragged a man outside and tried to knock him out by hitting him on the back of the head with his revolver; a shot was fired, unfortunately killing the horse that was tied to the tree next to the entrance.

Del Carril, Buenos Aires Province

page 19

El Farolazo 2006

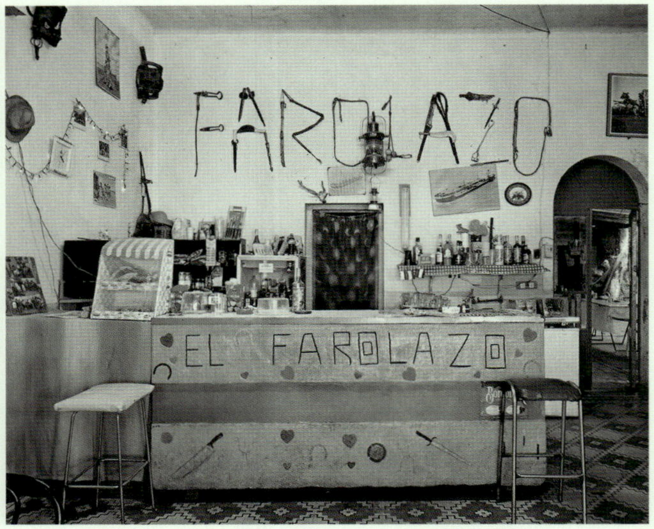

This is a bar whose clients are mostly people that work on the farms, hence the name on the wall written with farm tools. The word *farolazo* means "big lamp," and refers to the kerosene lamp that can be seen in the center of the photograph. Luis Enciso worked in the merchant marine for over thirty years, and this was one of the souvenirs he kept. After retiring, he bought a piece of property that included this old bar, so he restored it and ran it for a couple of years. He closed it when he felt too tired to continue.

Coronel Vidal, Buenos Aires Province

page 20

El Tropezón 2011

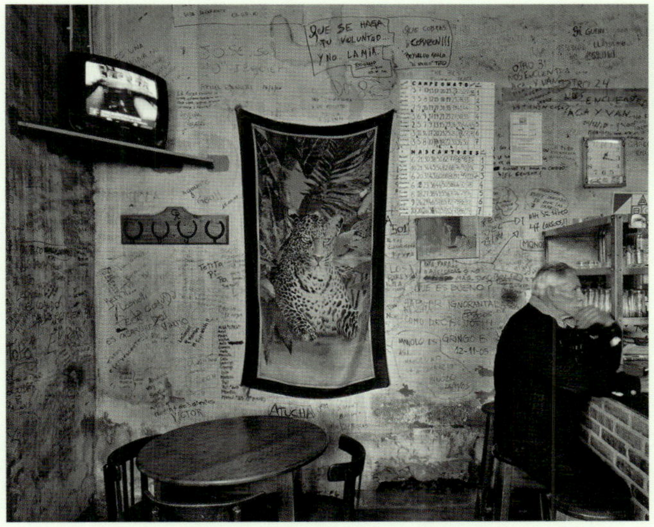

Many years ago, Carlos Rivero wrote a phrase on one of the bar walls out of sheer boredom. He was the owner, so he could do it. When the regulars saw it, they asked if they could do the same, and that's how they got filled. Twenty-five years ago, they repainted the whole bar, but soon enough, someone asked if they could write on the wall again, and he said "yes." The yellow tone is not paint but a mixture of moisture and cigarette smoke. The walls were originally painted white.

San Andrés de Giles, Buenos Aires Province

page 22

Bar Cacique 2005

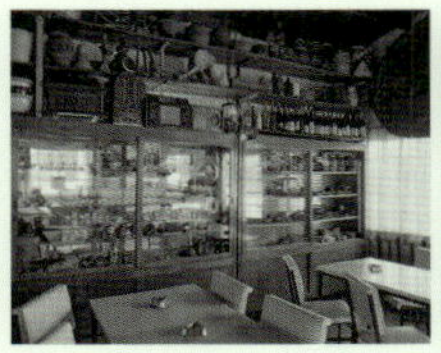

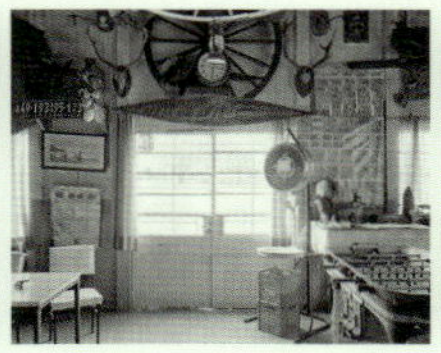

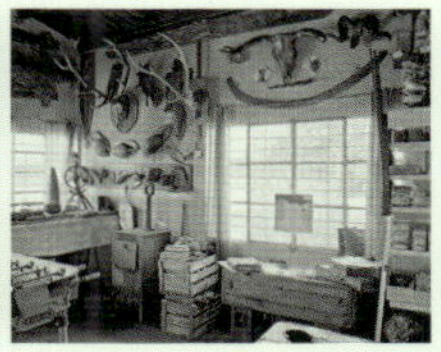

The Bar Cacique, to my eyes, corresponds directly to the concept of the cabinet of wonders. The owner, Omar Lescano, has always been interested in collecting random stuff such as snakes, taxidermy, animal parts, old currency, cigarette boxes, stones, guns, knives, and old radios. As word spread, his customers brought him personal donations that began to accumulate in the bar. When asked if he would be tempted to take something home, Omar responds, "These things don't belong to me."

Villa Cacique, Buenos Aires Province

page 24–25

Cuatro Esquinas 2013

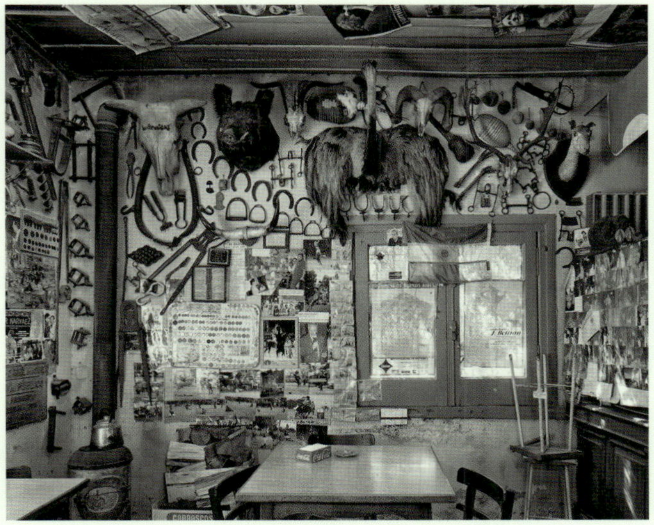

When Jorge took over Cuatro Esquinas, he had no idea what he was getting into. Middle-aged and with no previous experience, his background as a florist in the city didn't give him much hope. The hyperinflation of 1990s Argentina left him with nothing, so he had no other option but to take over the establishment, located thirty kilometers from the nearest town, in a crossroad. The night before opening, while he was cleaning up and arranging the merchandise, he thought to himself that this was the biggest mistake of his life. But he was proven wrong. The next morning, Jorge woke up early and went to unlock the door and open the windows. What he saw perplexed him: there were dozens of gauchos waiting outside, ready to have an early drink, get some food, buy provisions, or simply to socialize.

Rte 74 and Rte 30, near Tandil, Buenos Aires Province

page 27

Mira-Mar General Store 2014

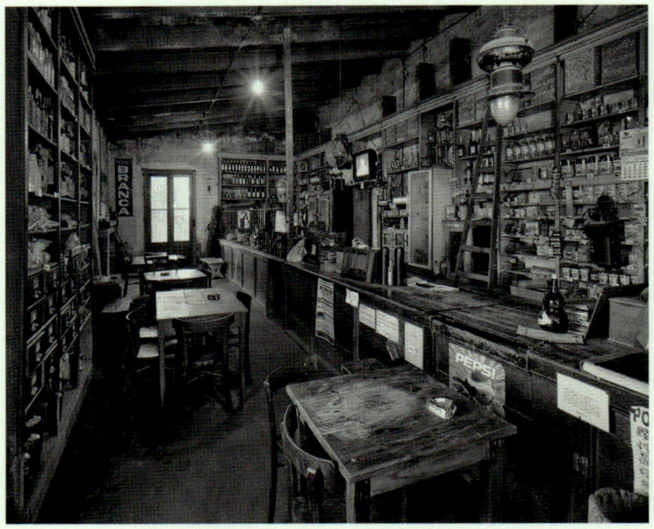

The Mira-Mar general store was opened in 1882 by Juan's great-grandfather. Just to get there one must drive over a sandy dirt road that meanders for about twenty kilometers, a trip that can discourage quite a few. Juan says he takes one day at a time, and organizes meals and traditional music and dance get-togethers in order to make some extra money to keep this old store from falling apart. His aging mother lives across the road from him, helping with what she can.

Near Bolívar, Buenos Aires Province

page 29

Langueyú General Store 2013

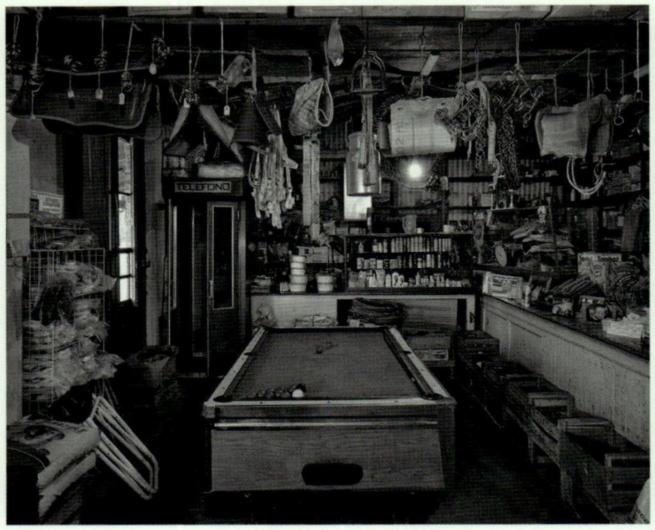

This old store is located in what is known as a *paraje*. This means that there are not enough people living there to consider it a small town. The customers are all farm-workers who will buy the basics, have a drink, play pool, and socialize. Beatriz and her father ran the business until recently, when he passed away due to a pulmonary disease. Now it's just her and she doesn't know if she will be able to manage by herself.

Langueyú, Buenos Aires Province

page 30

Chilecito Pool Table 2010

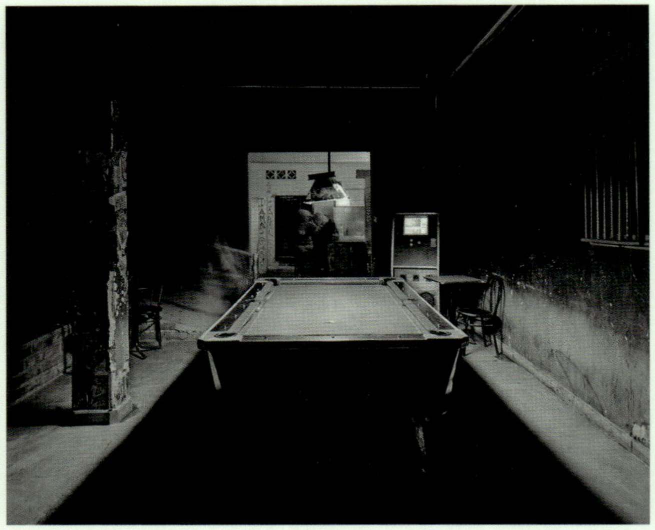

I drove past this bar in Chilecito and was drawn to the cave-like feeling it projected. The music was blasting and it was very dark. Men were playing pool and others sat at the bar drinking beer. I asked the bartender using exaggerated sign language if it was okay to take a picture and he gestured "Go ahead" with a head movement. I don't think they noticed when I left.

Chilecito, La Rioja Province

page 32

Bar Morena 2011

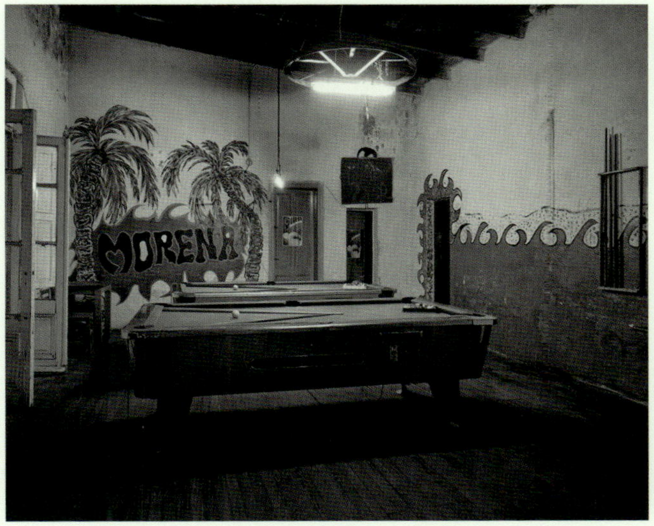

When I took this picture, the place was just starting out. The building was old but they were redecorating. Even though the bar is in a small town of about one thousand souls, it benefits from its proximity to large cities such as Lobos and Buenos Aires. The new owners were hoping this would work in their favor.

Uribelarrea, Buenos Aires Province

page 34

Bar Mangioni 2010

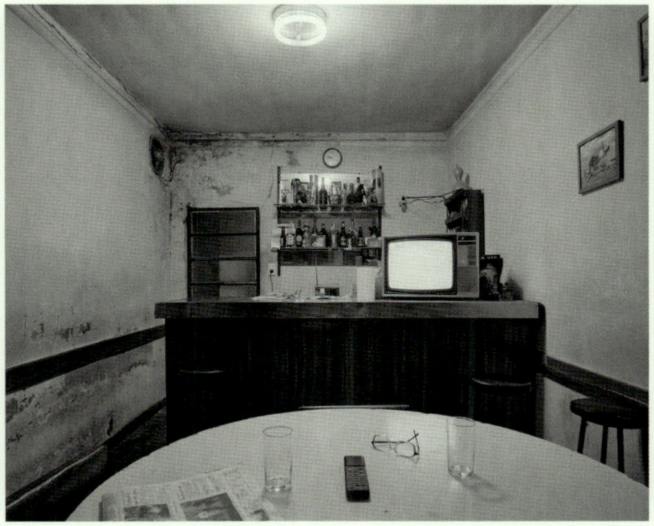

Before getting into the bar business, Mangioni organized a clandestine lottery. Because this turned out to be rather unstable and got him into trouble with the local police, he decided to buy this old bar, which he ran until he passed away. The place is now rented out as a grocery store. Although his son loved the bar, he also realized how much time it took from his father's life. He didn't want to follow the same path.

Coronel Dorrego, Buenos Aires Province

page 37

Casa Colo 2014

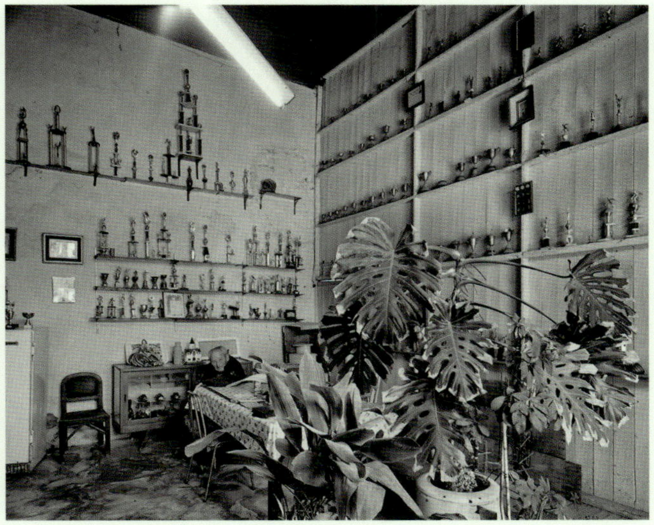

Colo lives by himself in an old house right in the center of the town of Laprida. It feels as if he doesn't belong to these times, or that he belongs exactly where he is and everything around him took a different direction. This room holds a collection of trophies that he has won for playing bocce and for target shooting.

Laprida, Buenos Aires Province

page 39

Casa Bolognani 2014

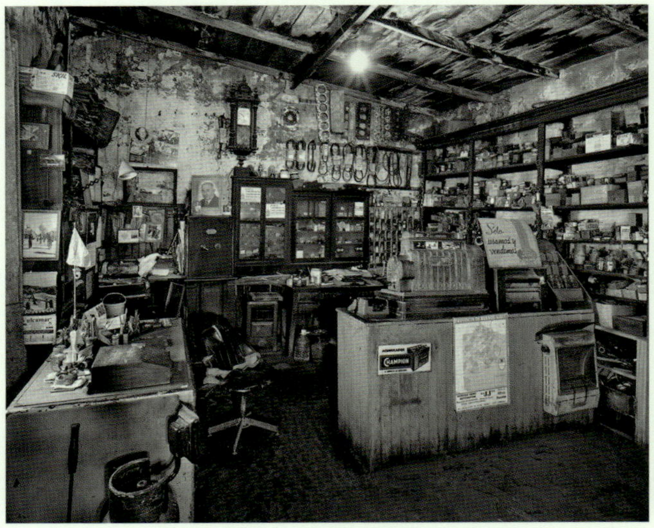

I drove into the small town of San Jorge right after lunch, at siesta time. I found a guy washing his car, so I got out and introduced myself, showed him my photographs, and asked if there was any old store "working as it used to be." He didn't hesitate and pointed me in the direction of Casa Bolognani. I drove four blocks and parked in the shadows next to an abandoned gas pump and napped until the shop opened. The floors were actually of stamped earth. I was happy to find out that Bolognani's son will continue once his father is gone, keeping alive this shop that also serves as a meeting point where locals can hang out and socialize.

San Jorge, Buenos Aires Province

page 40

Japón Dry Cleaners 2008

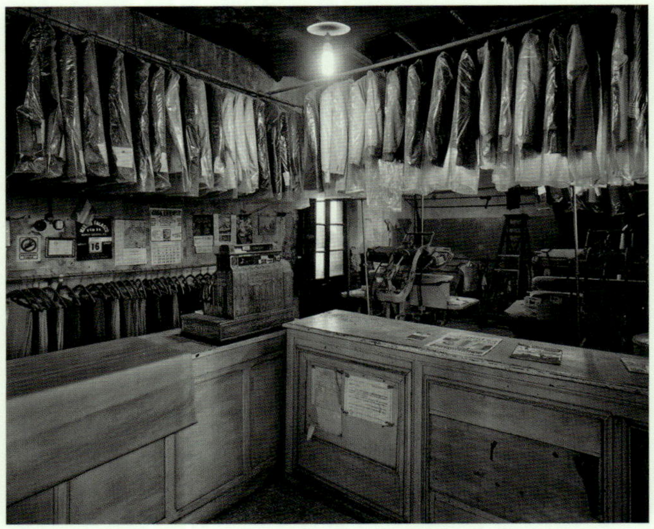

At the time I took the photo, Mr. Nakamurakare was very sick. Although he had stopped working, he would hang out at the shop reading the paper and keeping his son company. Two years after taking the picture, I called up to see if he was still around in the hope of interviewing him. His son explained over the phone that his father was under strict medical treatment and that it wasn't a good time, that I should try later, in a couple of months or even a year. Instead of waiting, I decided to stop by on a future trip. A couple of months had passed since our phone conversation. When I arrived I found that the place had been demolished. A rich businessman had bought the property and the Nakamurakares had moved to Buenos Aires.

Saladillo, Buenos Aires Province

page 42

El Ombú Fodder Shop 2008

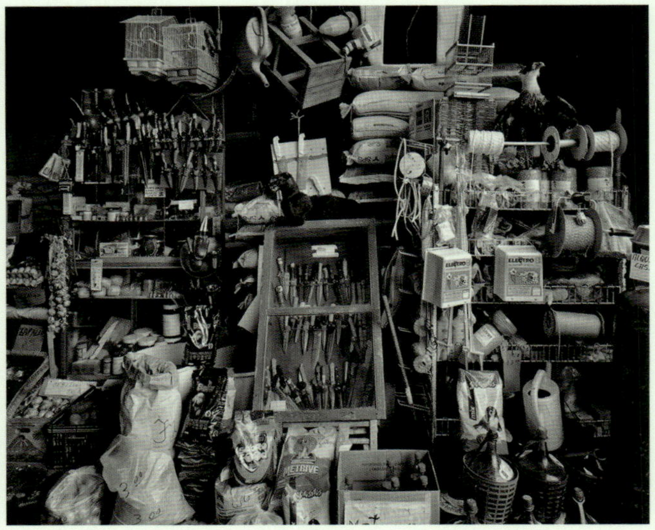

Pájaro ("The Bird") explained to me that his customers used to be mostly farm workers. Hence the fodder shop had a very rural, rustic feel. The live fish, taxidermy animals, knives, poison, feed, and electric wires were all piled up as if it were a barn. Since the clientele has shifted to a more urban type, this has recently changed, and the store has cleaned up quite a bit.

Saladillo, Buenos Aires Province

page 45

Sol De Mayo General Store 2009

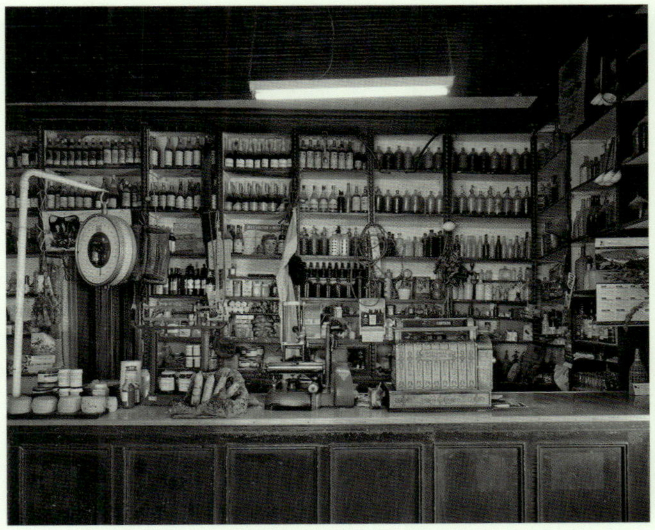

The couple living in Sol de Mayo used to be neighbors deep in the countryside. They fell in love and formed a family, and when their kids started growing up they decided to sell the farm and move closer to the town of Dolores so that the children could go to school. They bought this general store that dates from over a hundred years ago in order to be near the town while maintaining a rural lifestyle.

Rte 63, km 9, Buenos Aires Province

page 47

La Paz General Store 2009

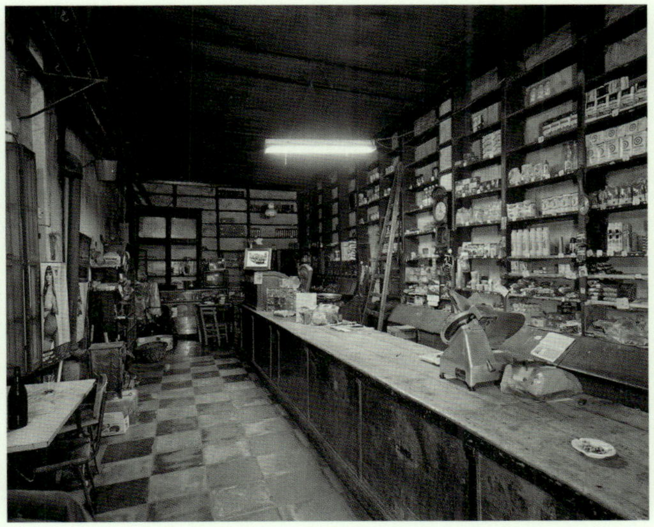

When I took this picture, Justo and Chola were running the La Paz general store. They were brother and sister. Ever since Justo died from an illness, Chola, who is in her eighties, has been left to attend the store all by herself. She said the two most important things to run this business were: first, don't owe money to anybody; and second, the real money is in serving drinks, not in selling food.

Roque Pérez, Buenos Aires Province

page 49

Tala General Store 2010

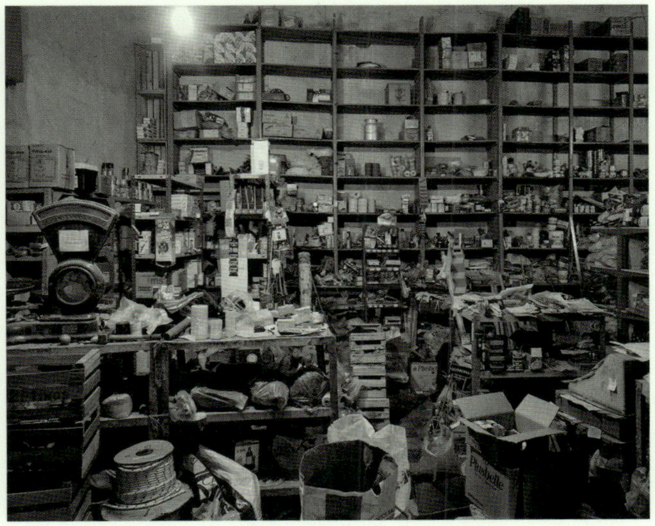

All I remember from this place was that while I was taking the picture, someone showed up with the produce from their plot and traded it for batteries. I asked later if that was a common thing here, and the answer was that some of the people in the area were so poor that it was easier to barter with them than having them owe money.

Jáchal, San Juan Province

page 51

Bar Firpo 2013

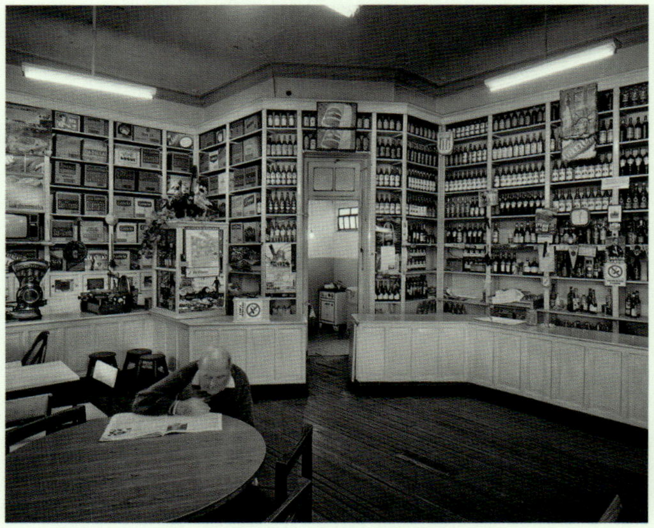

The Bar Firpo has had its regulars for many years, mostly old guys who would meet to play cards, read the paper, and watch TV, kind of like a social club. As the owner got older, in order to avoid future family confrontations he decided to sell the bar and divide the proceeds among his heirs. The night I returned with a copy of the photograph coincided with the night the guys were having their final toast before the bar closed for good. Whoever bought it decided to demolish it.

Tandil, Buenos Aires Province

page 52

Cardón Kiosk 2006

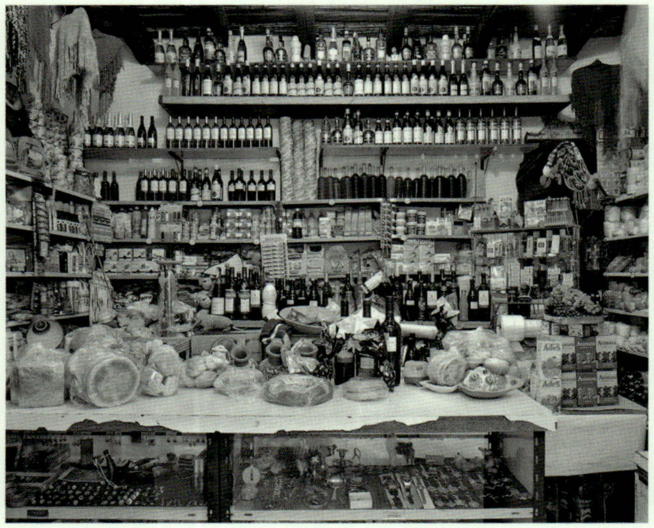

The Cardón Kiosk was quite recently established yet felt like it had been around for a long time. The mix of products that the owner had decided to include and exhibit was random: toys, jewelry, school utensils, clothing, bread, wine, cigarettes, homemade jam; everything seemed to fit within the confined space.

Cafayate, Salta Province

page 54

Campodónico General Store 2011

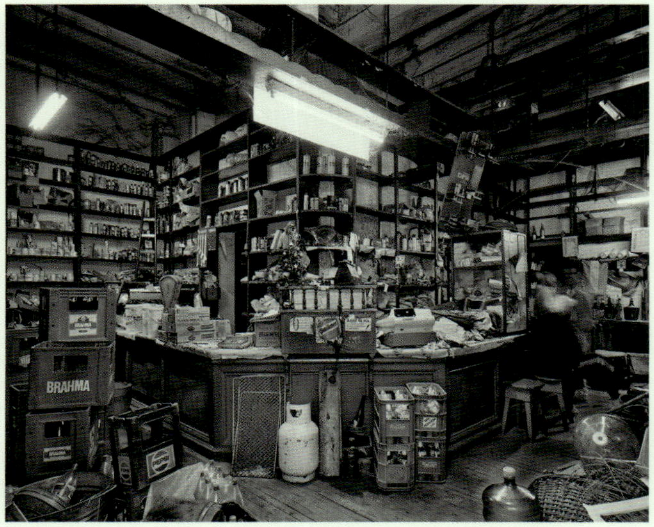

It is common for general stores to have a drinking section within the same space, but Campodónico felt different. Its decadence, in the best sense of the word, came from the strange mix of random products—tools, cookies, gas, spray paint—that would be sold next to the beer and other drinks. The last time I was there I found out the place had been closed for some time and no one could tell me if it would ever reopen.

Lobos, Buenos Aires Province

page 57

13 Hermanos General Store 2013

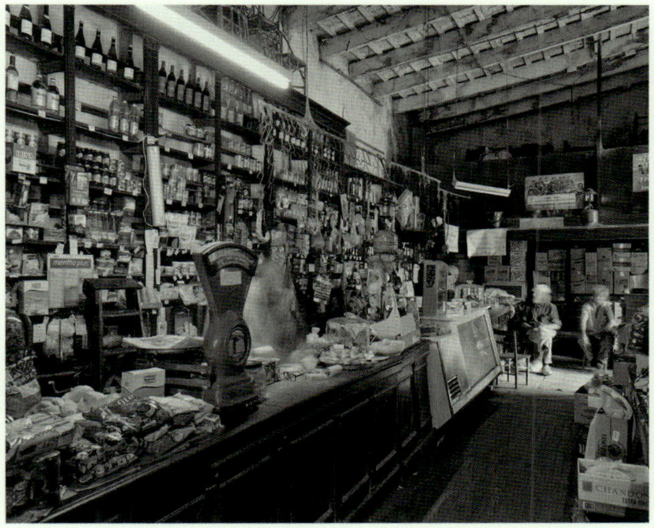

Norberto's grandfather founded the general store on March 13, 1915. That first night, he counted a total profit of 13 pesos, all in one-peso coins. So he named the store "13." Norberto Gregorio and his brother Alfonso Alberto have followed their father and grandfather's footsteps. They say that the number 13 has been recurrent in their lives; for example, their grandfather had 13 chickens when he first came here, and also they have an aunt that was born on a 13th, as well as a granddaughter.

Gouin, Buenos Aires Province

page 58

Adelfa's Market 2009

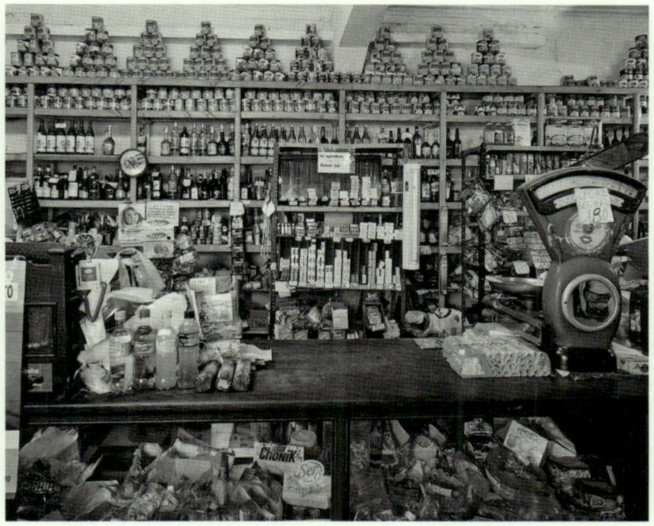

All her life Adelfa dreamed of running a food store. Her father worked at the train station and her mom was a washerwoman. She started at the market when she was seventeen and has continued for over forty-five years. Adelfa was upset when I brought her a copy of the picture because her cans were not as neatly arranged as they were in the photograph. She had had eye surgery and couldn't move much, so the place looked more disorderly than usual. She promised she would soon recover and straighten it up. Adelfa doesn't have any children and worries that no one in her family will be interested in running the market.

Lezama, Buenos Aires Province

page 61

Trecu Pharmacy 2013

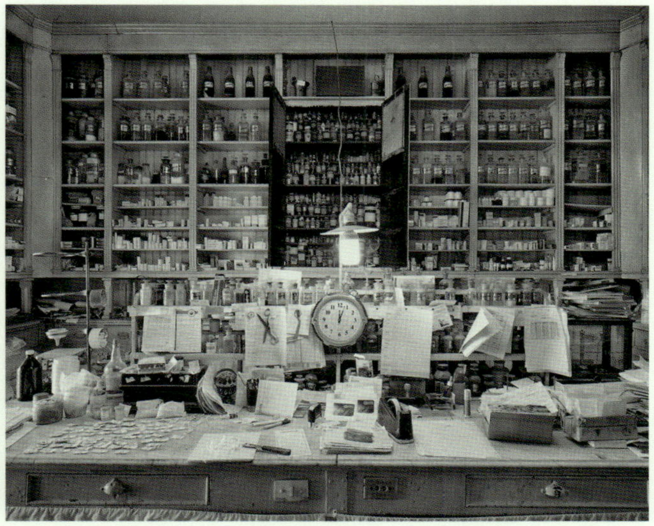

I remember many years ago I walked into the Trecu pharmacy and took a picture from the customer's point of view. The result was not particularly interesting, so I archived the negative. But seven years later, the Trecu Pharmacy popped into my mind again. I felt there was more to it, so I drove back to the town of Vela to ask Luis, the owner, if he would show me the room behind the counter, and he did. Directly behind that wall I had initially photographed lay this amazing space.

Vela, Buenos Aires Province

page 63

Town Barber 2013

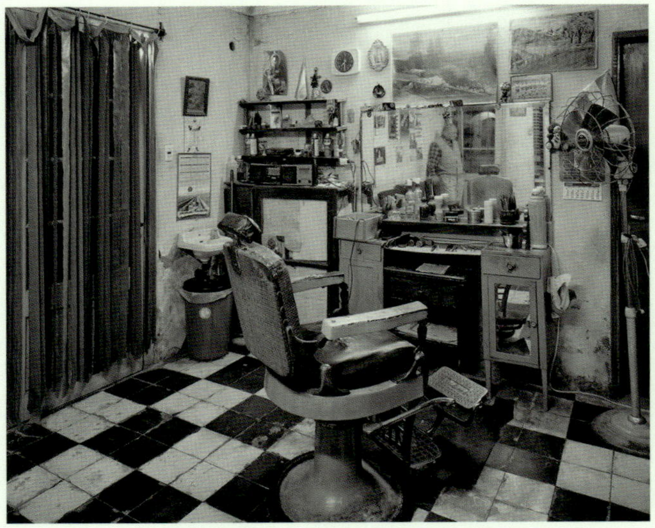

Alberto Ponce told me that he started off as a kid helping out in a big barbershop. There, he would clean the gentlemen's hats for tips. Back then people used to get a shave every three or four days, so it was very busy all the time. Alberto refuses to cut ladies' hair because he says they are too complicated in what they want. He keeps a small number of regulars who don't complain and he will not charge them if they can't pay. He says that at this point in his life, it's more a matter of keeping busy and entertained.

Rauch, Buenos Aires Province

page 64

"El 91" Butcher Shop 2006

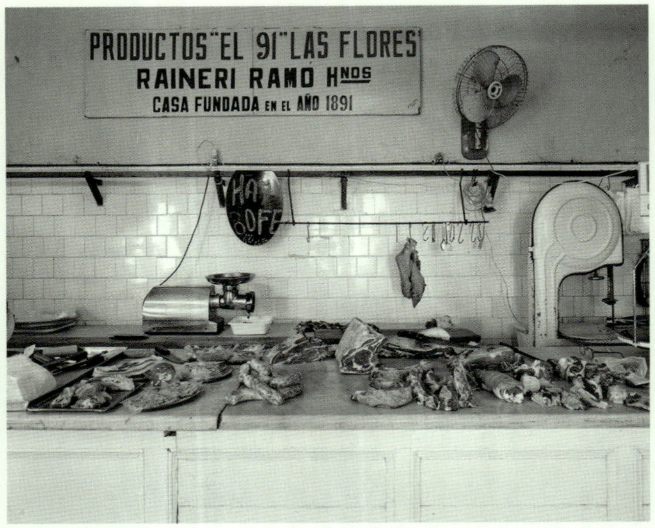

The "El 91" butcher shop doesn't exist anymore. Its owner, Juan Carlos, had been selling meat straight from the slab since he first started, more than sixty years ago. When new regulations demanded that he exhibit the meat cuts in a refrigerator, he realized, having no heirs, that it was time to close the shop. The investment was too high and he was too old. He died soon after.

Las Flores, Buenos Aires Province

page 67

Los Agapantos Pork Products 2014

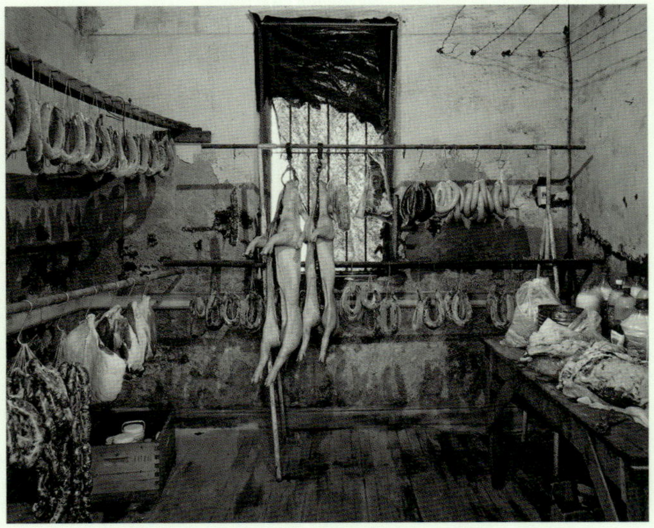

Norberto has been butchering all his life. Besides the actual slaughtered animal, he also produces sausage, chorizo, and liverwurst that he sells locally. The day I was taking the photo, he had three guys helping him with the killing and gutting of eight piglets and a large boar. They were very disorganized and one of the piglets managed to jump from the truck they were being kept in and ran away. By the time I left, they were still looking for him.

San Jorge, Buenos Aires Province

page 69

Sheep Rennets 2006

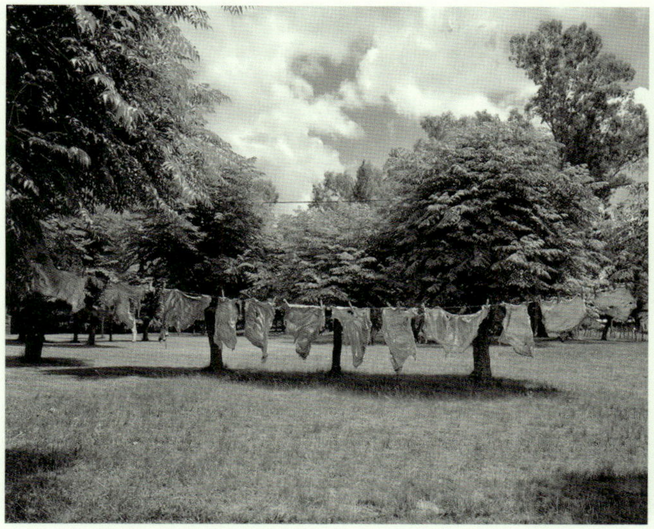

As I drove along Route 2 heading south, I noticed a clothesline with strange organic forms hanging from it. I turned around and headed over, intrigued to find out what it was. The gaucho living on that plot of land explained that the sheep stomachs, called *cuajos*, are used in making cheese. They needed to be dry before starting, so just like he did with his own clothes, he hung the dripping stomachs until they were ready.

Rte 2, km 41, Buenos Aires Province

page 71

Gauchito Gil Shrine, Route 34 2006

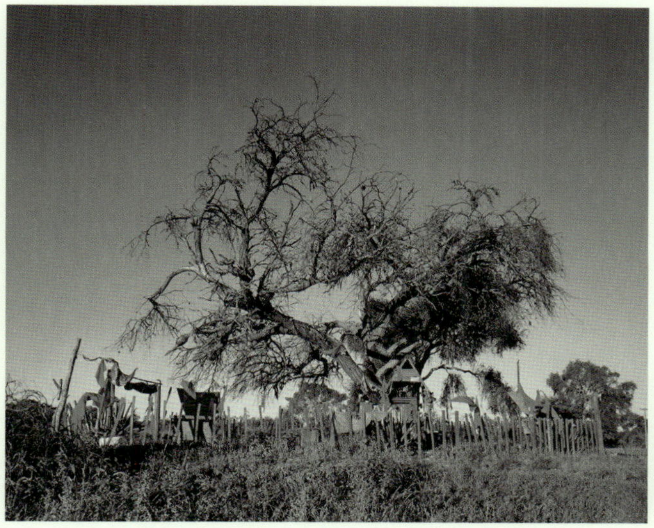

Shrines to the Gauchito Gil are often built under or near trees so as to be protected from the elements. The sun was coming down from a seamless blue sky as I drove through Santiago del Estero province. The scene felt perfect. It is amazing how these man-made interventions change the landscape and create such strange public installations. Anyone can walk up to the shrines and slightly modify them with an offering or a letter or an action.

Rte 34, km 568, Santiago del Estero Province

page 72

Gauchito Gil Shrine / Linden Tree 2005

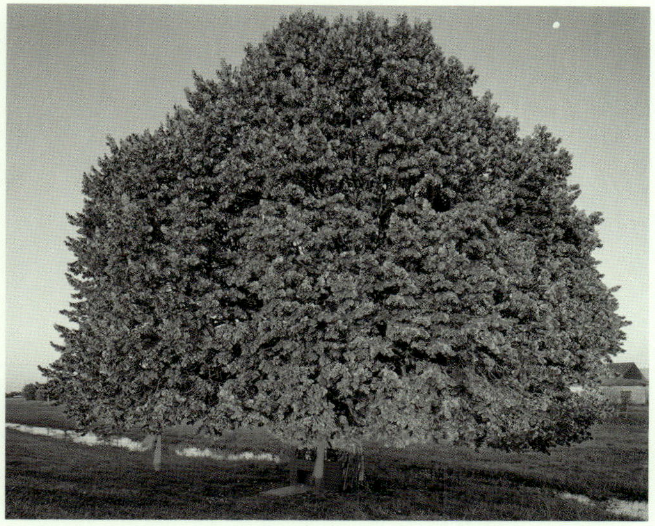

I took this shot at 6 a.m., when the sun was rising, and the reflection of the yellow light on the moving leaves created an effect that, combined with the shrine, made the whole scene come alive. I don't think I would have looked so closely at the linden tree if it weren't for the Gauchito Gil shrine underneath it.

Rte 3, km 495, near Tres Arroyos, Buenos Aires Province

page 74

Armadillo Shells 2007

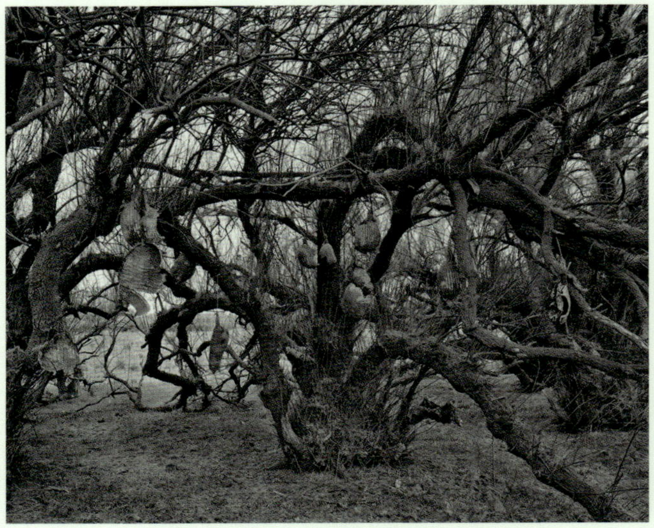

Rural homeless people are called *crotos*. They wander on the side of the highways or county roads until they choose somewhere to camp. Under this tamarisk tree next to a dirt road there was a *croto* living for a number of weeks. He told me he would feed himself from armadillo meat that he and his dog would hunt. The technique involved pouring boiling water into the animal holes and having the dog catch the armadillo as soon as it stuck his head out of the ground. He would hang the carcasses on the tree to dry so they wouldn't attract other animals. He was gone a couple of weeks after I took the picture.

Aparicio, Buenos Aires Province

page 77

Gauchito Gil Shrine, Route 51 2006

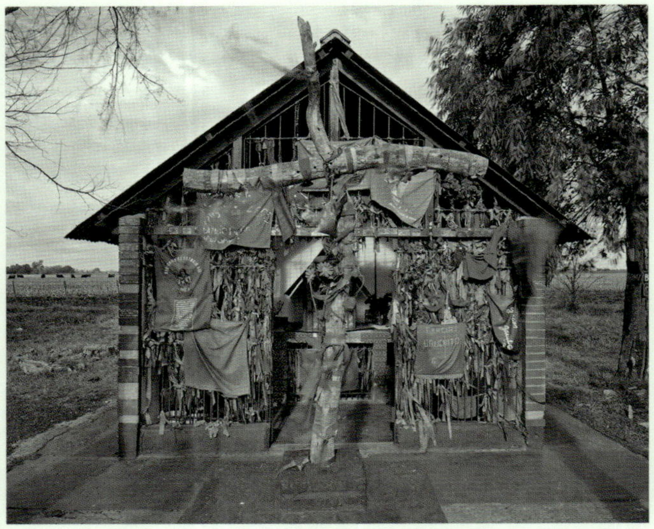

This particular shrine to the Gauchito Gil had been built in the middle of nowhere, close to a crossroad. Whoever did it knew what they were doing. The shrines are usually smaller and are placed under a tree or nailed to the trunk. The larger ones are not so common, and this one in particular felt well made. It is said that whoever builds a shrine does so in return for a miracle carried out. In the future, it is their responsibility to clean it and keep it presentable for other devotees.

Rte 51 and Rte 226, Buenos Aires Province

page 79

Gauchito Gil Museum 2006

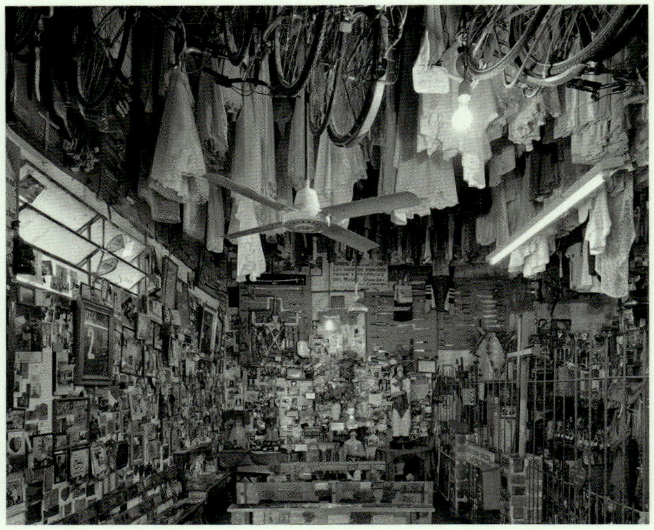

The Gauchito Gil is the most popular pagan saint figure in the country. In the late 1800s he deserted the army and became a persecuted outlaw. He wandered the province of Corrientes stealing from the rich and giving to the poor, like Robin Hood did. When he was caught, the sheriff decided to cut his throat. Gauchito Gil's last words were: "You are about to kill an innocent man. When you return home you will find your son dying. Only if you give me a Christian burial will he be saved." The sheriff gave the order to kill him and returned home, only to find his wife in tears and his son hallucinating in bed. He hurried back and dug a proper grave for the Gauchito, and, as promised, his son recovered. The legend of the Gauchito Gil still grows to this day, proof being this museum saturated with offerings, providing testimony to people's belief in his miraculous powers.

Mercedes, Corrientes Province

page 81

Difunta Correa Hermit 2010

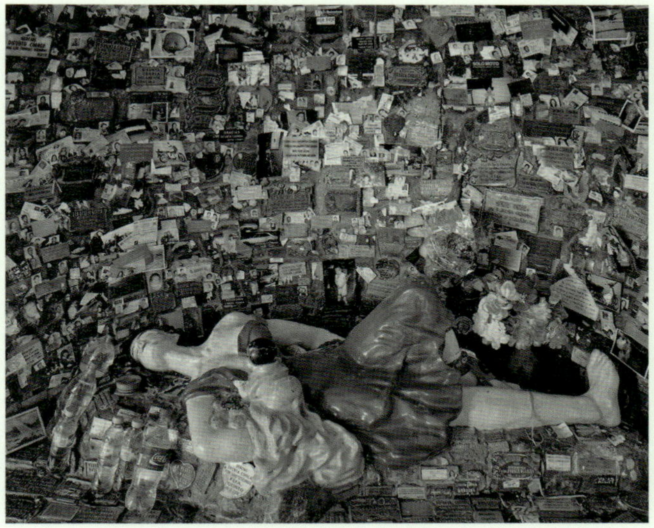

The Difunta Correa is one of the most popular pagan saints in Argentina. It is said that during the 1840 war between Unitarios and Federales her husband was forced to join the militia and sent off to La Rioja province, far from his family. Harassed by the local sheriff and heartbroken from the forced separation, Deolinda Correa took her newborn and attempted to cross the desert in search of her true love. Some days later a group of herdsmen found her lifeless body; she had died from dehydration but her baby had survived by drinking his mother's breast milk.

Vallecito, San Juan Province

page 82

Difunta Correa Shrine 2010

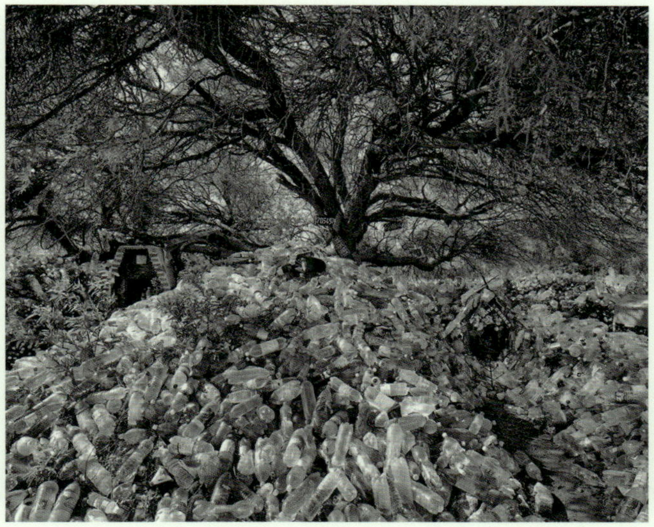

Shrines for popular saints appear in random locations throughout the country. You can tell if it's dedicated to the Difunta Correa because of the water-filled bottles that are left by her devotees. It begins with a few, then it slowly starts building until, at times, the shrine reaches unbelievable proportions.

Rte 38, km 106, Córdoba Province

page 85

Fernández's Garden 2006

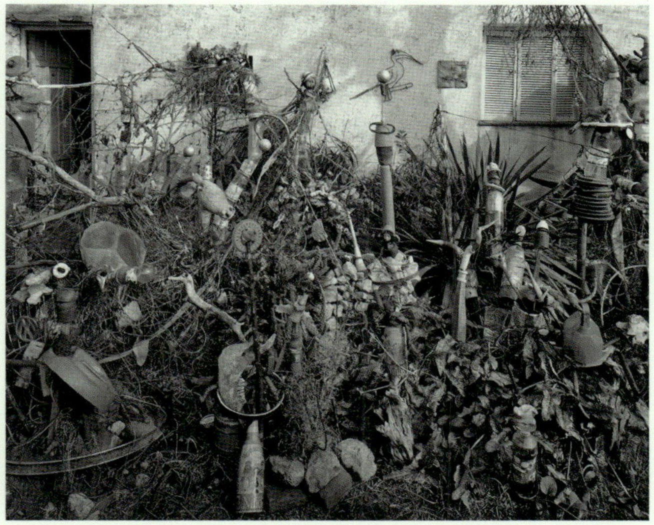

Mr. Fernández explained to me that he would go on long walks on the side of the highway collecting things that caught his eye and bring them home with him. There wasn't much more to it than that; he was a different guy, a "character" in the town. He said that when he ran out of money he would go to the hospital and sell his blood for a couple of days, then come back and live off the proceeds. Last time I was there, Fernández was gone and so was the garden.

Cascallares, Buenos Aires Province

page 87

Car Parts 2007

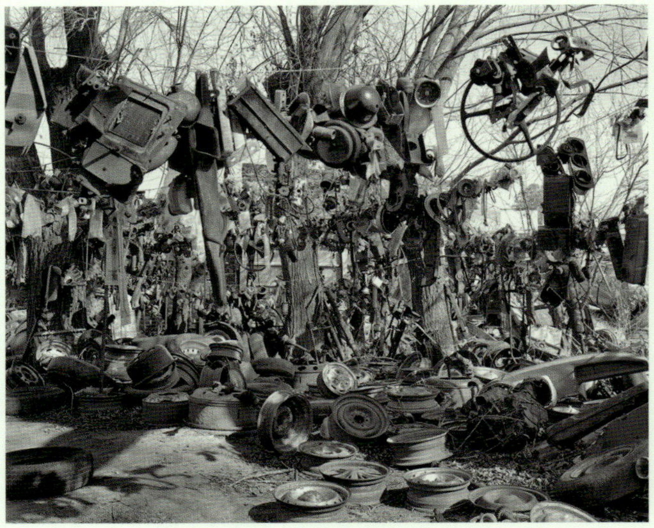

What first called my attention to this site was that it had no visible structure, no office, no shop, no shed, nothing. It was completely haphazardly built. Wires had been drawn between the trees and the parts had been randomly hung and organized around the perimeter. People would pull over on the side of the highway and walk around looking for a specific piece that just might be found in this organized junkyard. The place no longer exists.

Rte 205, km 185, near Saladillo, Buenos Aires Province

page 88

Difunta Correa Hangar 2010

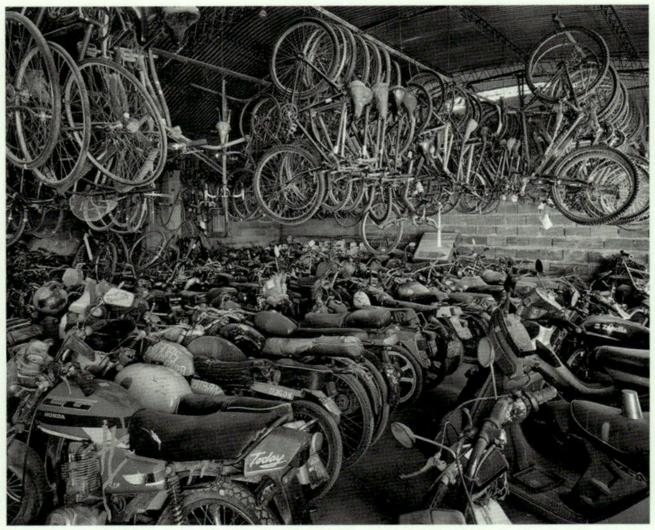

The main shrine of the Difunta Correa is a perimeter laid out like a small city. The paths connect several rooms and houses that exhibit the eclectic array of offerings that are brought each day by her devotees. One room is destined for clothes, another for paintings and drawings; there is one for toys, and this particular one for cars, bicycles, and motorcycles.

Vallecito, San Juan Province

page 90

"El Beto" 2013

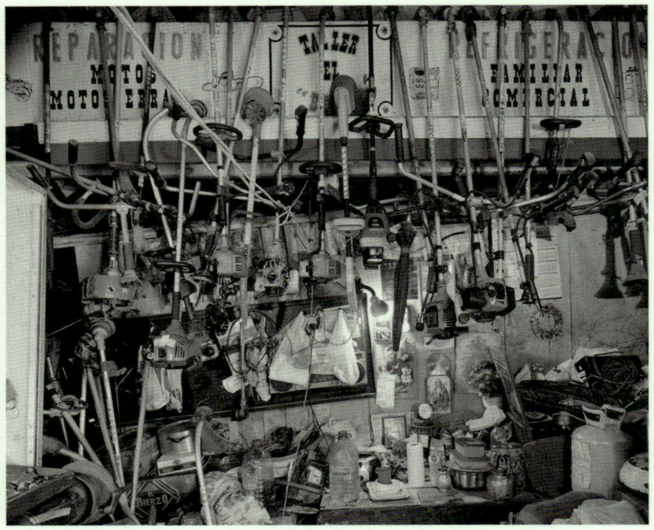

Beto has been fixing small engines for as long as he can remember. This shop has been active for fifty-seven years. Many customers will leave their broken engines to be fixed and might pick them up three or four years later, if ever. Beto cannot sell or get rid of them, so they keep accumulating in the shop.

Capilla del Señor, Buenos Aires Province

page 93

Grierson Refrigeration 2013

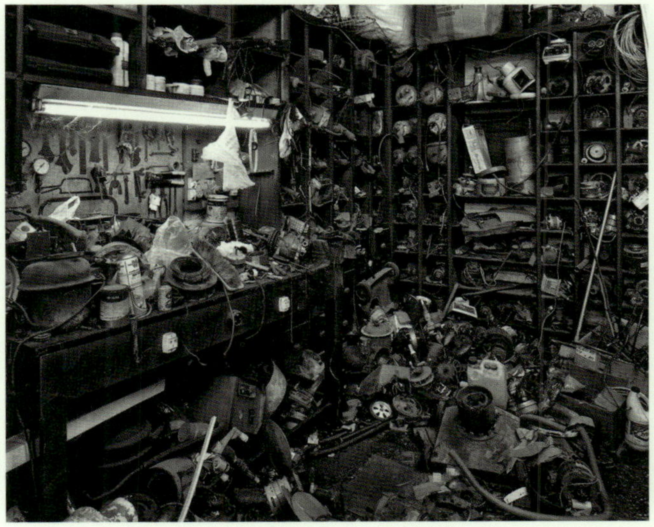

Someone from another town told me that if I was looking for messy interiors, this was the place to go. Grierson's is dedicated to restoring and building air conditioners, refrigerators, and cooling chambers. When I walked into the shop they said I was lucky, that the week before they had actually done some cleaning up. Grierson swears he knows exactly where each part is in his shop.

Rauch, Buenos Aires Province

page 95

Fulgenci Shoe Repair 2013

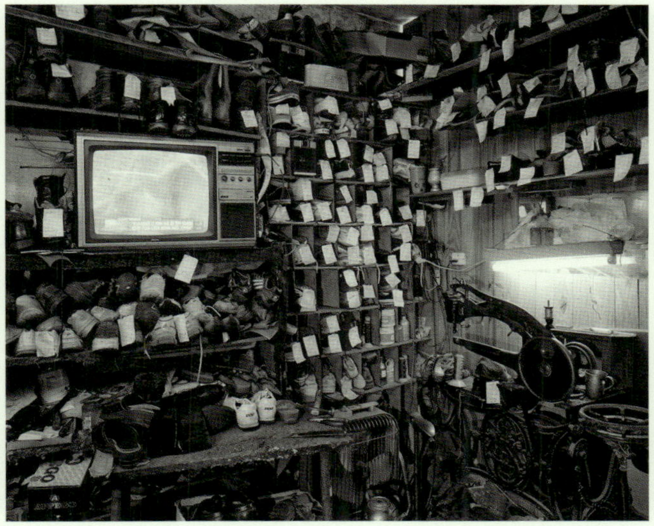

I drove past the Fulgenci shoe repair shop and had a feeling there was more to it than what I could see from the street. I walked in and introduced myself, showed Mr. Fulgenci my photos, and bluntly asked if I could take a look behind the wooden wall that separated the shop from the counter. The back of the shop reminded me of a morgue, each label identifying the shoe with its owner. I asked if he could turn on the TV to add more feel to the place, and he did. It took about ten minutes for the tubes to warm up, but it worked fine. He was proud of having seen the 2010 World Cup on that old television.

25 de Mayo, Buenos Aires Province

page 97

Ceferino's Workbench 2014

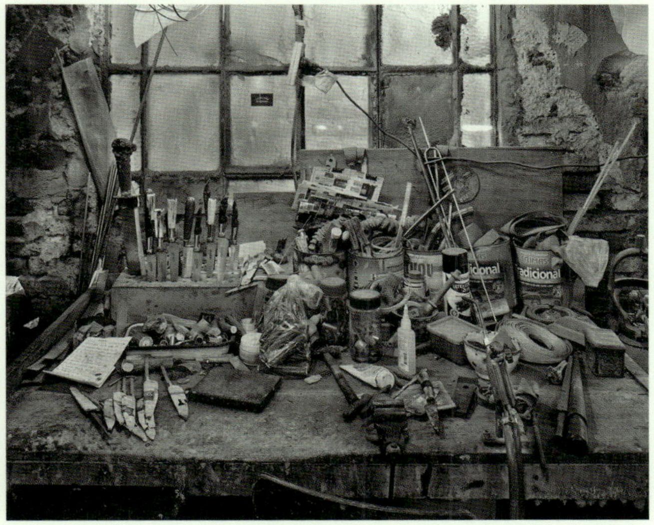

Ceferino is the eldest and most experienced worker at the 3H knife factory. His job is the final assembly before the knife leaves the shop. He will put together the right blade with its proper handle and make sure that it is sturdy and well balanced. All details—joints, welds, finishes, etc.—are checked by him before he sends them on to the store.

Tres Arroyos, Buenos Aires Province

page 98

Yunque Knife Factory 2014

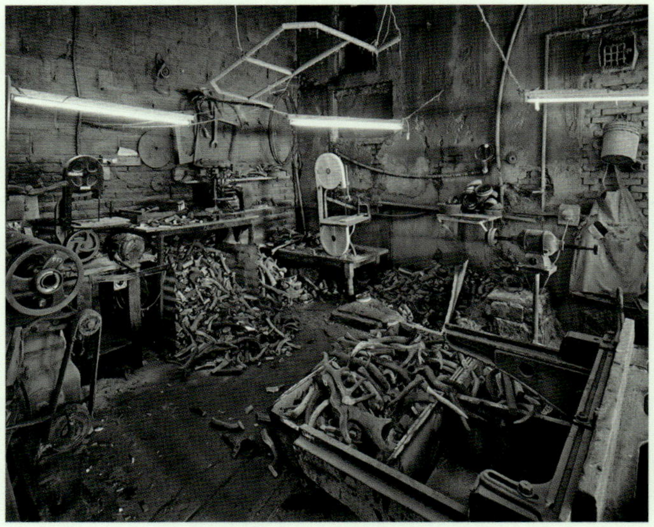

The shop is covered in a thin dust that comes from the debris from cutting and polishing deer horns. Because they are bought from a game preserve, no animals are hunted for this purpose. Deer horns make beautiful and effective knife handles. They can also be made out of wood and animal parts such as armadillo tail or ostrich fingers.

Tres Arroyos, Buenos Aires Province

page 101

Ismaelito's Welding Shop 2013

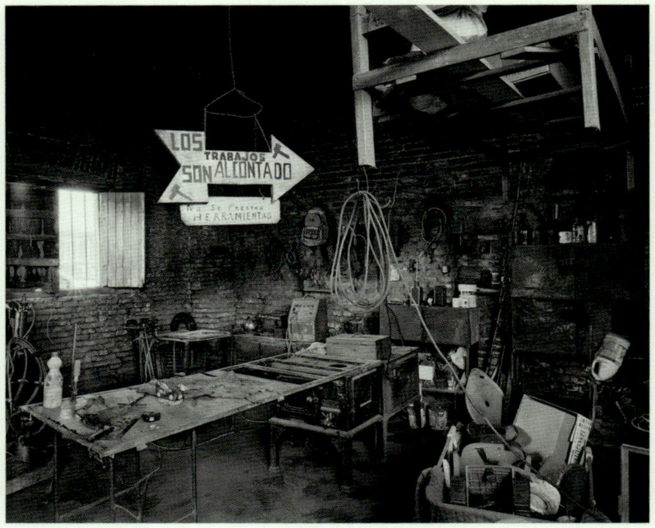

I found Ismaelito because I was told his welding shop was the oldest in town. I knocked on his door and a tiny old man poked his head out of a cut-out window. I told him I was a photographer and that I wanted to see the inside of the building. I am always amazed at how generous people are in the small towns, letting me into their places of work, sometimes their homes, without knowing me. The signs inside the shop read: "All jobs are cash only" and "We do not lend out tools." Ismaelito's father believed those were the two most important precepts to properly run a welding shop.

Ayacucho, Buenos Aires Province

page 103

La Estrella Bakery 2014

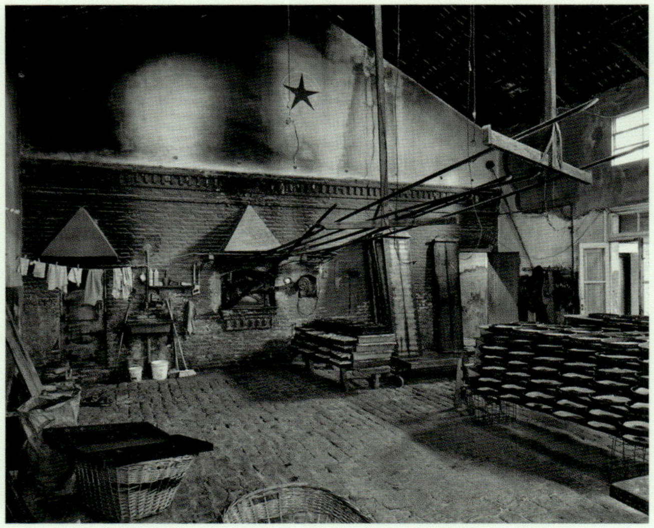

This bakery produces enough bread and dough for the owner to drive forty kilometers each day to deliver to the larger town of Laprida. The town of San Jorge has two hundred inhabitants. It was on my second visit that I was able take the photograph, since on my first visit, Hugo, the owner, was on delivery and the person in charge was not comfortable letting me in. On this occasion, the sun was coming down and there was hardly any light left.

San Jorge, Buenos Aires Province

page 105

Marcelino López General Store 2009

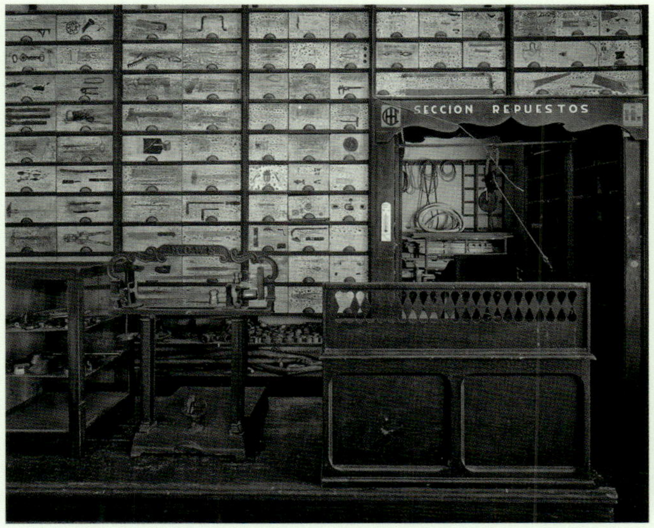

As I drove through the long main road that leads to Indio Rico, I noticed an old corner that caught my eye. I got out of the truck and took a peek through the window. The place looked half empty and there was no one inside. Then I saw a truck pull behind the building, so I went over and introduced myself. It was one of the owners. He told me the place had closed some months prior, but he was willing to open it for me to take the picture. I was drawn to the rusty shadows of tools and parts fossilized into the drawers. It was a beautiful statement on the passage of time.

Indio Rico, Buenos Aires Province

page 106

Leili Bike Shop 2010

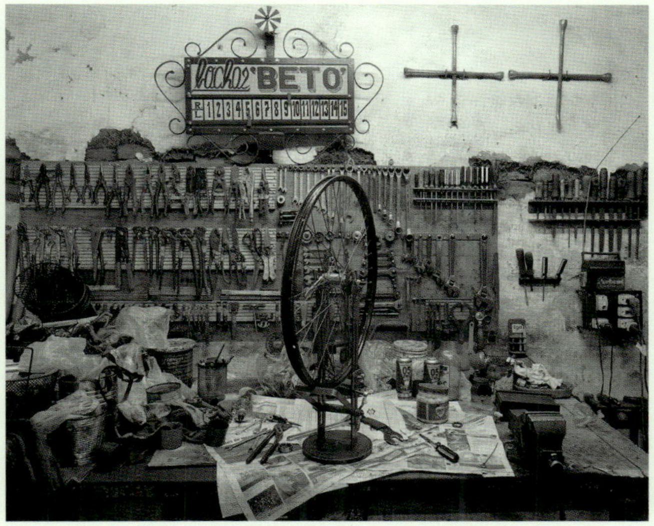

Alberto Lind retired as a police officer and had to find something to do in his spare time, so he opened a bicycle repair shop. His family complains about how dirty the shop is, in part because the building is made of adobe. They want him to close and move to his garage. Alberto understands that part of his tranquility comes from the fact that he is not at home all the time.

Moisesville, Santa Fe Province

page 109

Luis's Chainsaw Repair Shop 2013

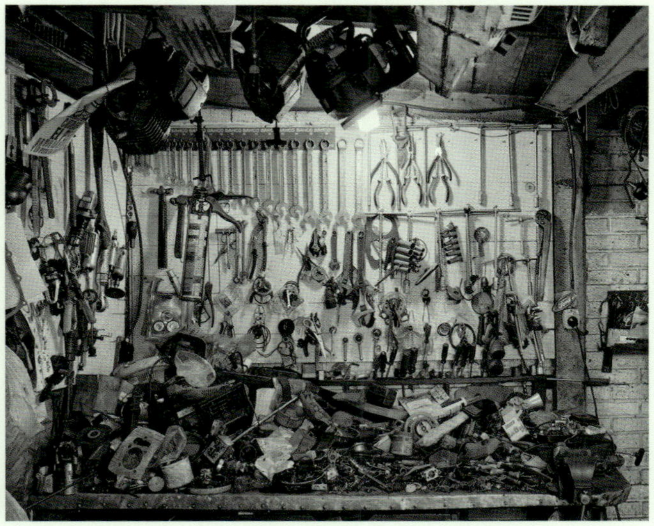

I met Luis when I stopped him on the street and asked for directions. It had been a while since my last find and I was getting anxious to take another photograph. I opened my portfolio and told him I was interested in old stores and shops that were messy and full of stuff. Just by chance, it turned out he was a chainsaw mechanic. He invited me in and it turned out to be the perfect chaos.

Ayacucho, Buenos Aires Province

page 111

Raúl's Tire Repair Shop 2010

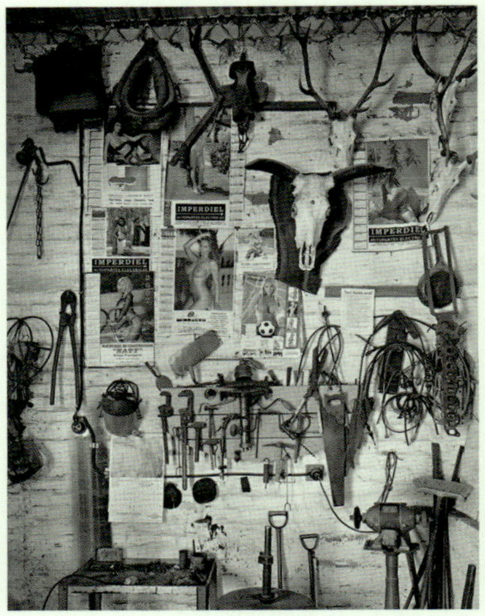

Raúl considered himself a collector, and many of the tools and objects hanging on the walls in his tire repair shop were merely decorative. He was a single dad and his teenage daughter was hanging out in the shop with him. The interior was wallpapered with posters of half-naked girls mixed with his antiques, while outside the young boys from the town gathered with their motorcycles and four wheelers courting the young teenager.

Luan Toro, La Pampa Province

page 113

Beto Cejas Rope Maker 2013

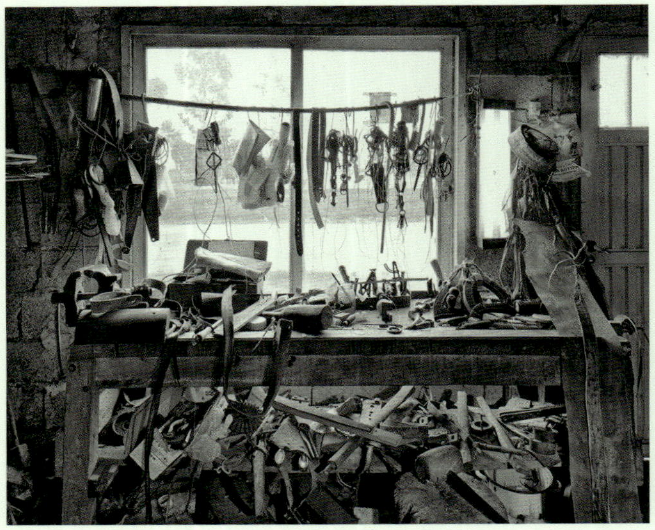

Beto Cejas explained the different ways of his trade. How diverse leather was and how many things he could do with it. It starts with the tanning of the hide, which he does in his backyard. Then the leather is cut in a spiral shape, from the inside out, in order to obtain the rope. Everything is done by hand, and he can make basically anything out of it, even the string he uses for stitching the parts together.

Laprida, Buenos Aires Province

page 114

Colonna Wood Shop 2009

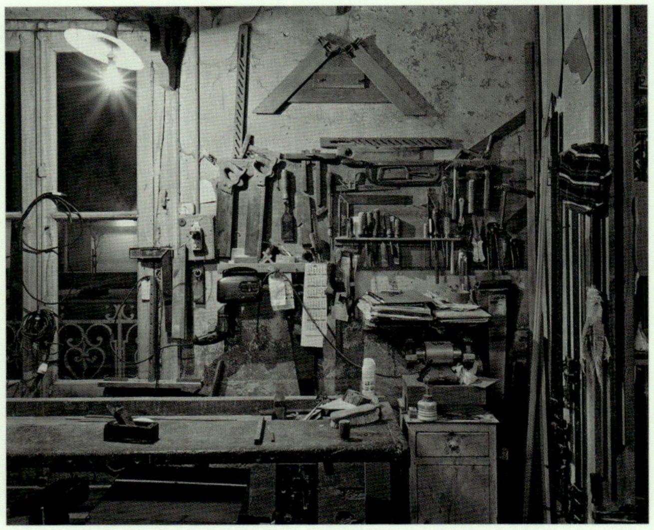

Miguel Colonna learned the trade when he was a kid. He didn't like to study so he dropped out of school and began as an apprentice in a wood shop around the corner from where he lived. Paradoxically, when he grew up he ended up as a teacher in a trade school. For the first class meeting he would begin by saying, "Wood is always present in our lives. When we are born, we are put in a cradle made of wood, and when we die, we are put in a coffin made of wood. It's a material that follows us through our entire lifetime."

Oriente, Buenos Aires Province

page 116

Rivero's Carpentry Shop 2013

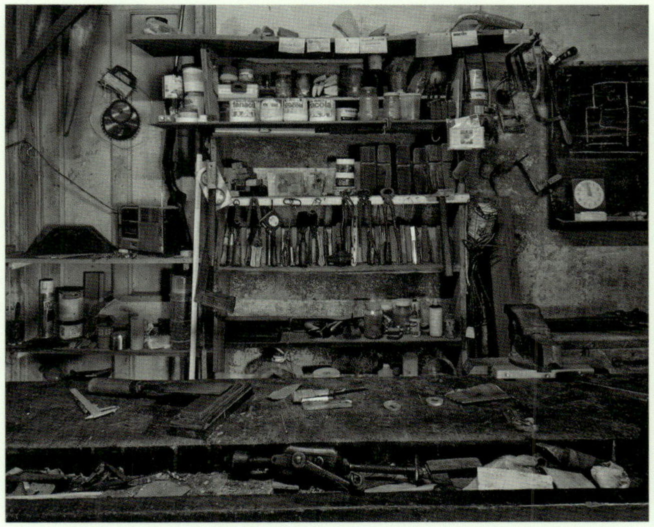

There was this corner I kept seeing in the town of Ayacucho that haunted me. Every time I drove by, the shutters were down. I found out that it was a carpentry shop, so it made me even more eager to find my way in. I asked around and was told that the owner was a "bohemian," a term used to describe artistic and solitary people, that he would frequent the bar down by the main square, and that his name was Rivero. I drove to the bar and asked for the bartender. He told me Rivero was taking care of his ailing uncle and that I would be lucky to find the shop open. He pointed out to me that Rivero rode a blue women's bicycle. He even offered to give me his home address, but I thought that was going too far. I drove to the shop one last time and, as if I had invoked him, there it was, the blue women's bicycle leaning against a tree.

Ayacucho, Buenos Aires Province

page 118

El Resorte Upholstery Shop 2014

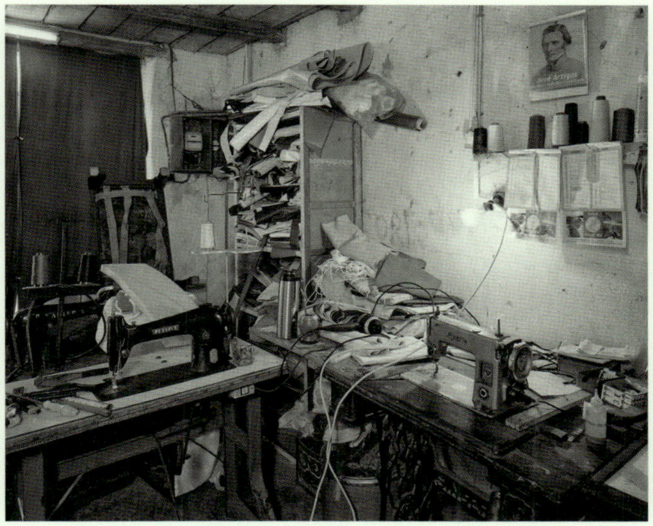

Yvonne found out she was an upholsterer by chance. When she was in her twenties, a friend asked if she could accompany her to buy some furniture. While at the store, her friend pointed out a particular piece, to which Yvonne answered that she thought it was poorly made. She didn't feel the finishing was right. What Yvonne didn't realize was that the salesperson had overheard her. She looked at Yvonne and said, "You are right. Can you make a nice set of pillows for me?" She said yes, although she didn't even know how to sew a button. Two months later, thinking Yvonne knew what she was doing, the saleswoman showed up with a big job for her. At first, Yvonne panicked, but then she put her mind to learn the trade, and that's how she became an upholsterer.

San José, Uruguay

page 121

El Triunfo Tinsmith Shop 2014

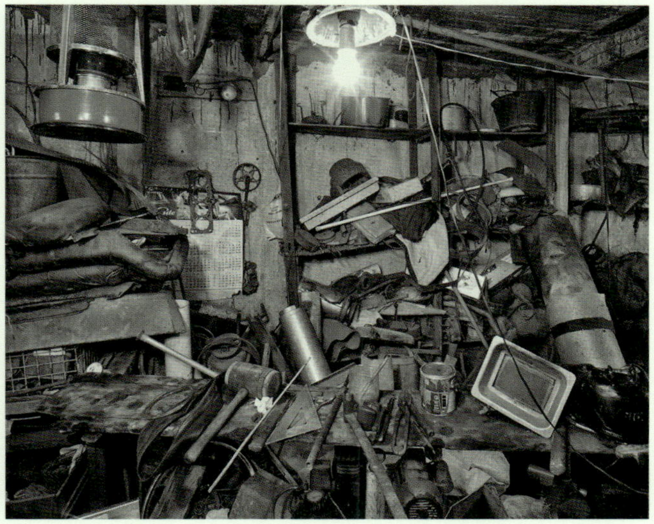

I was traveling in Uruguay and asked around the small town of San José if there were old tradesmen still around. Someone pointed me to a tinsmith, which made me excited since I had never photographed one before. After circling around, I found the man, but he had retired. Yet he pointed me to a colleague of his; I was to recognize the shop because of all the scrap and junk piled on the sidewalk. Indeed, I had no doubts when I pulled over that I had found the tinsmith. I asked Dario, the owner, what exactly a tinsmith does, and he explained that it was mostly artisanal jobs, the most common of which were general roof work, ducts for wood-burning stoves, and containers for feeding chickens and hogs.

San José, Uruguay

page 122

La Cueva 2013

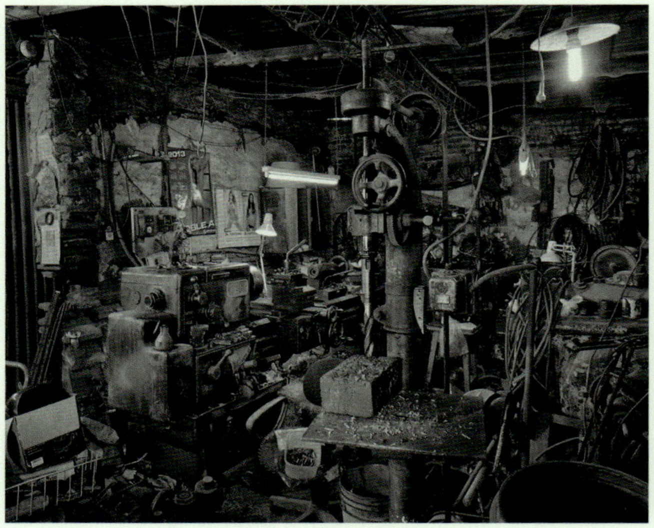

One of the things I remember the most is Juan García's theory about what to do when things get complicated in the welding shop. He said that whenever he felt blocked, he would stop what he was doing and go out to his backyard where he kept bunnies and had a vegetable plot. He would feed and talk to the bunnies, spend some time with them, water the plants, clear his mind, and then go back to work. This way, the problem would be resolved much easier.

Capilla del Señor, Buenos Aires Province

page 124

Pelado's Welding Shop 2013

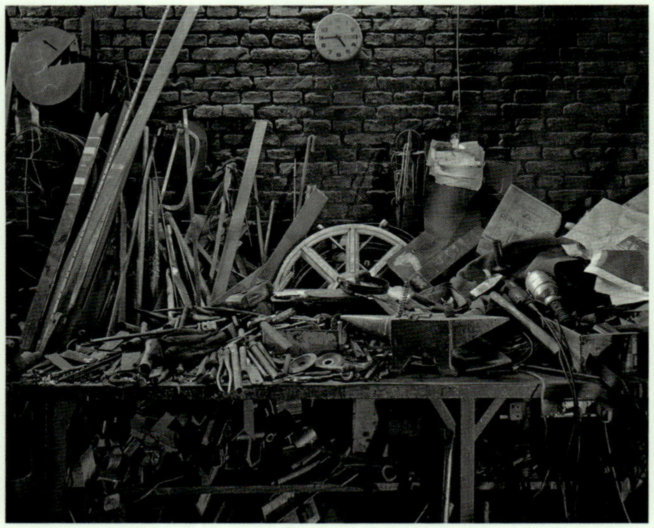

I walked into an old car shop where two old men were chatting and drinking maté. After showing them my photographs, one of them asked me, "You're looking for trash and disorder? You want a welding shop?" "Yes, that would interest me," I replied. The old man told me to look for "El Pelado," and gave me directions. The town's historic welder greeted me with a smile and had no problem with me taking a picture. There was hardly any space to put my tripod down and I had to move some metal scrap and other detritus in order to position myself behind the camera. In a strange balancing act, I managed to take the picture, or so I thought. Back in Buenos Aires, after processing and scanning, I realized I had left part of the anvil out of the frame. In Roland Barthes's terms, I had chopped off the punctum, the one object that held my attention over the rest. El Pelado scratched his scalp when, three weeks later, I showed up at his gate asking if I could take another picture.

25 de Mayo, Buenos Aires Province

page 127

García's Broom Making Shop 2013

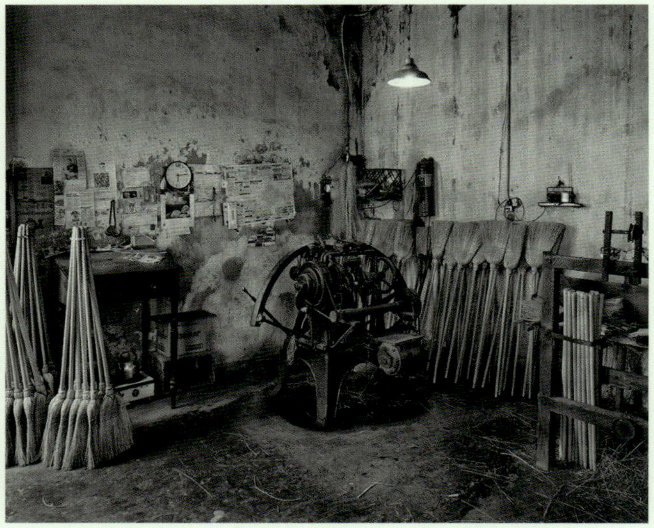

Mr. García told me he was having problems with his trade. For one thing, the materials were hard to find, since, to my surprise, there are different brooms that require different straws. He was upset because people were buying cheap imports rather than his handmade products. There was also another problem, which was that García needed someone to help him in the shop, and he told me that his apprentices would last no more than a couple of weeks. So he had given up trying to teach the trade. Twice I drove out to visit him, and on both occasions the shop was closed. I am still trying to find him.

Chivilcoy, Buenos Aires Province

page 129

Tucho's Sign Painting Shop 2010

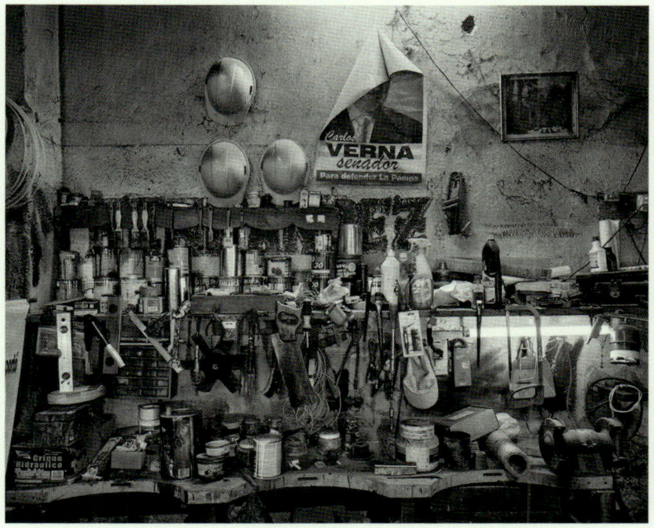

Tucho was part of a group of regulars having a drink at Bar El Mate in La Pampa. After I convinced the owner that I wasn't a tax collector, everyone got interested in looking at my photos. He then saw me photograph the bar, and eventually asked me if I would be interested in seeing his shop, which was three doors down from the bar. I think he got a little jealous of his neighbor.

Uriburu, La Pampa Province

page 130

Lathe 2013

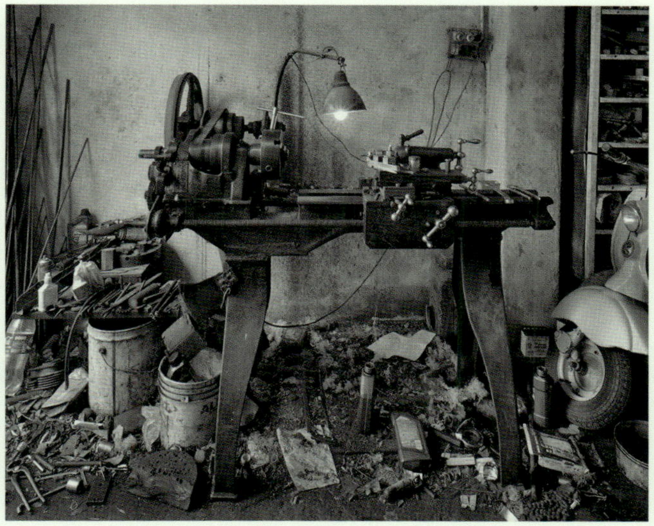

Inside Liuzzi's shop I found this beautiful lathe. It had an animal-like presence. The marks of burned metal on the wall and the scrap underneath made me think that it had a life of its own, as if, after years of being in that space, it had expanded and taken over a larger territory.

Ayacucho, Buenos Aires Province

page 133

Faienza's Shop 2014

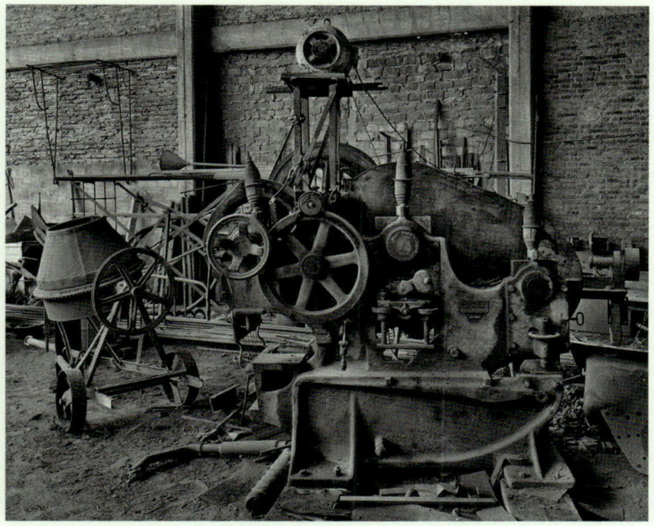

This machine was originally brought from Germany to help build the railroad system. When the company went bankrupt, Mr. Faienza bought it and dragged it with a truck over the asphalt to his shop. It was so heavy it dented the street pavement. Now it is used to cut thick pieces of metal such as beams for hangars and other large buildings.

Tres Arroyos, Buenos Aires Province

page 135

Visit www.srodekhart.com to listen to the people behind the photographs telling their stories.

Acknowledgments

Robert Sadler, "el Viejo Vizcacha," for making me a wiser and a better man. Jim and Jacquie Dow, for your love and generosity throughout all these years. Alfons Hug, for putting me in touch with the right kind of people. Ben, Hannes, and Jill from Kuckei + Kuckei Gallery, this book wouldn't have happened without you. I will always be grateful for this opportunity.
Anne Wilkes Tucker, thank you for your valuable contribution to this book. Curt Holtz and everyone at Prestel for making something difficult seem easy. Julia Ramos, for being at my side through this ride. My teachers at the School of the Museum of Fine Arts and the Massachusetts College of Art and Design, Laurel Reuter and the folks at the North Dakota Museum of Art, Kent Rodzwicz for your patience and advice, EP Levine, especially Jill MacLeod and Shawn Plouffe, Molly Toberer, Bruce Berman, Kai Loebach, Barbara Ruben, Dudu von Thielmann and Jean-Louis Larivière, Martha Schneider, Joe Carroll, Dina Mitrani, Jennifer DeCarlo, Arlette Kayafas, Mark Elliott, Heidi and Steve Aishman, Alejandro Barbosa, Arti, Pablo Dragovetsky, Florencia Szapira, Kela Merino, Rodolfo Sauco, and my family, especially Mom, Dad, and Oma.

My deepest appreciation goes to those who let me into their shops, bars, stores, and homes.

This book is dedicated to Federico Hart.
I will always remember you.

Prestel Verlag, Munich
A member of Verlagsgruppe Random House GmbH

Prestel Verlag
Neumarkter Strasse 28
81673 Munich
Tel. +49 (89) 4136-0

Prestel Publishing Ltd.
14-17 Wells Street
London W1T 3PD
Tel. +44 (20) 7323-5004

Prestel Publishing
900 Broadway, Suite 603
New York, NY 10003
Tel. +1 (212) 995-2720

www.prestel.com

Library of Congress Control Number: 2014958072
British Library Cataloguing-in-Publication Data: a catalogue record for this book is available from the British Library; Deutsche Nationalbibliothek holds a record of this publication in the Deutsche Nationalbibliografie; detailed bibliographical data can be found under: http://www.dnb.de.

Prestel books are available worldwide. Please contact your nearest bookseller or one of the above addresses for information concerning your local distributor.

Editorial direction: Curt Holtz
Editing: Hannes Kuckei and Jill Leciejewski, Berlin
Copyediting: Jonathan Fox, Barcelona
Production: Astrid Wedemeyer
Design: Peter K. Koch, Berlin
Origination: Reproline Mediateam, Munich
Printing and binding: DZS Grafik, d.o.o., Ljubljana

FSC www.fsc.org MIX Paper from responsible sources FSC® C110418

Verlagsgruppe Random House FSC® N001967
The FSC®-certified paper GardaPat Kiara
is produced by Lecta.

ISBN 978-3-7913-8144-2

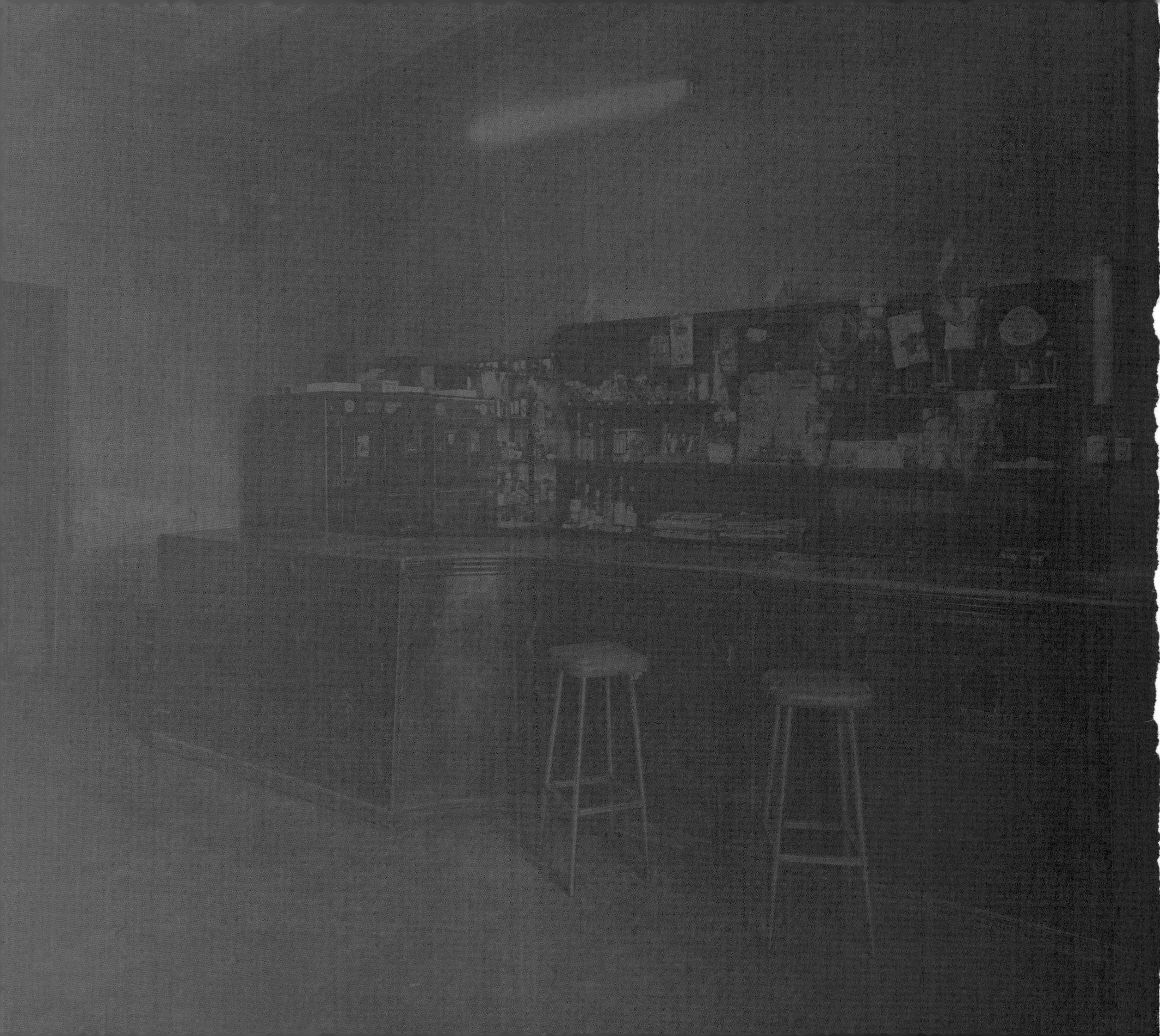